Hyper-V Best Practices

Equip yourselves with the real-world configurations
and best practices of Hyper-V to take full advantage
of its virtualization capabilities

Benedict Berger

BIRMINGHAM - MUMBAI

Hyper-V Best Practices

First published: November 2014

Production reference: 1211114

Published by Packt Publishing Ltd.
Livery Place
35 Livery Street
Birmingham B3 2PB, UK.

ISBN 978-1-78217-609-1

www.packtpub.com

Cover image by Charlie Mather (matherc@yahoo.com)

Credits

Author

Benedict Berger

Reviewers

Benjamin Armstrong

Andreas Baumgarten

Shannon Fritz

Carlo Mancini

Charbel Nemnom

Carsten Rachfahl

Commissioning Editor

Taron Pereira

Acquisition Editor

Shaon Basu

Content Development Editor

Shaon Basu

Technical Editors

Tanvi Bhatt

Mrunal M. Chavan

Kunal Anil Gaikwad

Copy Editors

Roshni Banerjee

Janbal Dharmaraj

Karuna Narayanan

Project Coordinator

Mary Alex

Proofreaders

Simran Bhogal

Maria Gould

Ameesha Green

Paul Hindle

Julie Jackson

Graphics

Disha Haria

Abhinash Sahu

Indexers

Monica Ajmera Mehta

Priya Sane

Production Coordinator

Komal Ramchandani

Cover Work

Komal Ramchandani

About the Author

10 years ago, Hyper-V MVP **Benedict Berger** started working with Microsoft Virtualization Solutions. Especially with the first beta version of Windows Server "Longhorn", there were many new features he wanted to try out immediately. "I was particularly interested in Hyper-V, but at that time, there was hardly any experience on this topic, especially in German-speaking areas. Therefore, I had to work out many solutions on my own, and since then, I have been sharing the knowledge I gained with much more intensity and reach. I founded the German Hyper-V Community together with two friends a couple of years ago to promote this topic in Germany even further," he explains.

He currently works as a solution consultant for Elanity Network Partner GmbH. Elanity is an IT-service provider that specializes in cloud enablement in Germany. In this dream job, he helps his customers to adjust their IT solutions to their own business processes and to deploy "real" dynamic private and public clouds instead of just virtualizing some systems. So, the tools of his daily work are Windows Server with Hyper-V, System Center, and Microsoft Azure. Before joining Elanity, he worked for a German financial service provider and the global car giant Volkswagen in similar functions.

He is a regular speaker at global conferences such as System Center Universe DACH, E2EVC Virtualization Conference and Microsoft TechEd as well as local conferences such as the TechNet Conference in Berlin, in which more than 500 experts participated.

He blogs on the German Virtualization Blog (http://blogs.technet.com/b/germanvirtualizationblog/) and on his personal blog (http://blog.benedict-berger.de). He is also the creator of the PDT GUI, a graphical user interface for the PowerShell Deployment Toolkit.

Acknowledgments

First of all, I have to thank my wife, Carina, for being there for me, every time, and making this book possible.

I thank the whole community for contributing best practices to Hyper-V and evolving the experience around a great virtualization solution. A special thanks goes to the folks at Microsoft and my fellow Hyper-V MVPs who have spent a lot of time each day to make this solution a perfect one.

A huge thank you goes to my reviewers for contributing a lot of time to ensure the quality of this book, especially Benjamin Armstrong, Lead Program Manager of Hyper-V, who is so busy creating the next version of Hyper-V but still took his time to improve this book. However, every reviewer, including Andreas Baumgarten, Carsten Rachfahl, Shannon Fritz, and Carlo Mancini did a great job ensuring this book's quality!

I thank my employer, Elanity Network Partner GmbH, and my bosses, Peter Schröder and Andreas Waltje, for allowing me the time and resources to support the Hyper-V community and making projects such as this book real.

I also thank my great team of coworkers at Elanity, especially Natascha Merker, who actively supported me through writing this book. Kamil Kosek has to be mentioned too for his great PowerShell skills, ensuring a high degree of automation.

Last but not least, I thank the great team at Packt Publishing for creating this book, accepting me as an author, and offering great support through the process of writing.

About the Reviewers

Benjamin Armstrong is a principal program manager working on Hyper-V at Microsoft. He has spent over a decade working on virtualization technology and is known as the "Virtual PC Guy".

Andreas Baumgarten is a Microsoft MVP and works as an IT Architect with the German IT service provider, H&D International Group. He has been working as an IT professional for more than 20 years. Microsoft technologies have always accompanied him, and he can also look back on more than 14 years' experience as a Microsoft Certified Trainer.

Since 2008, he has been responsible for the field of Microsoft System Center technology consulting, and ever since has taken part in Microsoft System Center Service Manager 2010, 2012, and 2012 R2; additionally, he has participated in the Microsoft System Center Orchestrator 2012 and 2012 R2 technology adoption programs with H&D.

With his in-depth technology know-how and his broad experience across the Microsoft System Center product family and IT management, he now designs and develops private and hybrid cloud solutions for customers all over Germany and Europe.

In October 2012, 2013, and 2014, he was awarded the Microsoft Most Valuable Professional (MVP) title for System Center Cloud and Datacenter Management.

Andreas is a co-author of *Microsoft System Center 2012 Service Manager Cookbook*, *Microsoft System Center 2012 Orchestrator Cookbook*, and *Microsoft System Center 2012 R2 Compliance Management Cookbook*, all by Packt Publishing.

Shannon Fritz is a Microsoft MVP for Enterprise Security and is the Cloud Datacenter Solutions Architect and the Team Lead at Concurrency, Inc.; a system integration consulting firm focused entirely on Microsoft solutions. He specializes in Windows Server platform solutions, including Hyper-V, Remote Desktop Services, DirectAccess, and a plethora of other services. Shannon holds an array of Microsoft certifications, including MCP, MCSA, MCITP, and MCSE. An active blogger, Shannon has also been a technical reviewer on other publications, including *Microsoft DirectAccess Best Practices and Troubleshooting, Packt Publishing*.

On a personal note, I want to thank my wife, Megan, whose incredible patience and encouragement inspires and motivates me. Her expectation of the best in all things reminds me that each decision in life has implications, both short and long term, and keeping focused on your goals will ultimately be rewarded. You are the reason our kids are so amazing. I love you, and thank you! Also, thank you to the wonderful organization Concurrency, Inc. What an amazing group of people that collectively lift each other up. I'm so glad I took that step into consulting with you!

Carlo Mancini has been working as a system administrator for over 15 years and on PowerShell since its first release in 2007.

Over time, he has developed high-level skills and achieved many different certifications, such as VCP5, MCSE, MCDBA, and HP Openview Certified Consultant.

He is one of the winners of the 2013 PowerShell Scripting Games and is currently employed by one of the largest European IT companies where he is in charge of maintaining and administering both the physical and virtual architecture.

He is recognized worldwide, thanks to his involvement in delivering excellent content on many technical forums as well as on his blog, www.happysysadm.com.

Charbel Nemnom is a Microsoft Most Valuable Professional (MVP) for Hyper-V and a team leader with IT infrastructure expertise, and has a vast knowledge of a variety of Microsoft technologies. He has over 13 years of professional experience in the IT field and guiding technical teams to optimize performance of mission-critical enterprise systems. He has worked as a system and network engineer, as a senior consultant, and as an IT manager, and has a history of successful enterprise projects in the IT, banking, education, and publishing sectors. He began working with Microsoft Hyper-V Server with version 1 back in 2009, and has focused on Microsoft virtualization ever since. He works for SABIS® Educational Services in the Gulf region as a regional IT technical manager.

He is a Hyper-V geek and also runs his blog at `http://charbelnemnom.com`, where he blogs frequently about Hyper-V and System Center for the Hyper-V Community.

He is a Microsoft Certified Solutions Expert and holds credentials such as MCP, MCSA, MCTS, MCITP, MCS, and MCSE. You can also follow him on Twitter at `@CharbelNemnom`.

I would like to dedicate a big thank you to my family, and especially to my wife, Ioana, for her support and patience throughout this project, who is the reason that I can fulfill my dream and follow my passion.

And last but not least, I want to thank the Packt Publishing team for supporting all the authors and reviewers during this project.

Carsten Rachfahl started his IT career in 1988, working as a developer on porting X-Windows to an operating system called OS/9. In 1991, he founded his own company in Germany and has been self-employed ever since. Starting 2001 with Citrix/Terminal server, his focus was on the virtualization space. When Microsoft finally created a "real" hypervisor and brought that to the market, he was all in. His blog, `http://www.hyper-v-server.de`, is highly recognized and appreciated within the virtualization community. The blog features tutorials, articles, screencasts, video interviews, and podcasts focusing on the Microsoft Private Cloud. Being MCT, he teaches various Microsoft virtualization courses, as well as his own "Hyper-V Powerkurs" course. As the co-founder of the German Hyper-V Community, he regularly organizes events. Carsten is a well-know speaker at conferences in Germany and Europe. His efforts were rewarded with the Microsoft MVP Award for Hyper-V in 2011, 2012, 2013, and 2014.

I want to thank my wife, Kerstin, and my kids, Ian and Ina, for the ongoing support, their understanding, and encouragement. Without you guys, I could not follow my passion.

www.PacktPub.com

Support files, eBooks, discount offers, and more

For support files and downloads related to your book, please visit www.PacktPub.com.

Did you know that Packt offers eBook versions of every book published, with PDF and ePub files available? You can upgrade to the eBook version at www.PacktPub.com and as a print book customer, you are entitled to a discount on the eBook copy. Get in touch with us at service@packtpub.com for more details.

At www.PacktPub.com, you can also read a collection of free technical articles, sign up for a range of free newsletters and receive exclusive discounts and offers on Packt books and eBooks.

https://www2.packtpub.com/books/subscription/packtlib

Do you need instant solutions to your IT questions? PacktLib is Packt's online digital book library. Here, you can search, access, and read Packt's entire library of books.

Why subscribe?

- Fully searchable across every book published by Packt
- Copy and paste, print, and bookmark content
- On demand and accessible via a web browser

Free access for Packt account holders

If you have an account with Packt at www.PacktPub.com, you can use this to access PacktLib today and view 9 entirely free books. Simply use your login credentials for immediate access.

Instant updates on new Packt books

Get notified! Find out when new books are published by following @PacktEnterprise on Twitter or the *Packt Enterprise* Facebook page.

Table of Contents

Preface

Hyper-V Server and Windows Server 2012 R2 with Hyper-V provide best-in-class virtualization capabilities. Hyper-V with the second generation VMs have security enhancements, less time to boot the OS, speed up OS installations, and automatic activation of VMs. There are many more enhancements in R2, which will give the developers reasons to rejoice. This book will equip you with the real-world Hyper-V configurations and best practices to take full advantage of its virtualization capabilities.

What this book covers

Chapter 1, Accelerate Hyper-V Deployment, starts with pointing out the ideal installation method of Hyper-V hosts and then goes on to introduce automatic VM models.

Chapter 2, High Availability Scenarios, covers the creation of a Hyper-V Failover Cluster and configuration of its best practices.

Chapter 3, Backup and Disaster Recovery, starts with the backup methods of Hyper-V hosts and VMs, and continues with Hyper-V Replica as a disaster recovery component in Hyper-V.

Chapter 4, Storage Best Practices, details the different storage scenarios possible with Windows Server 2012 R2 and Hyper-V.

Chapter 5, Network Best Practices, covers the different network virtualization scenarios possible with Windows Server 2012 R2 and Hyper-V.

Chapter 6, Hyper-V Performance Tuning, explains the fundamentals of performance management and tuning in Hyper-V.

Chapter 7, Management with System Center, describes the management of Windows Server with Hyper-V through various System Center components.

Chapter 8, Migration to Hyper-V 2012 R2, covers the migration to Hyper-V 2012 R2 from other hypervisors or earlier Hyper-V versions.

What you need for this book

To utilize all the configurations shown in this book, you should use the Windows Server 2012 R2 on a physical server system either as a trial or full version. You can also use the freeware edition of Hyper-V Server 2012 R2.

Who this book is for

This book is intended for those who already have some basic experience with Hyper-V and now want to gain additional capabilities and knowledge of Hyper-V.

If you have used Hyper-V in a lab environment before and now want to close the knowledge gap to transfer your Hyper-V environment to production, this is the book for you!

This book is not intended as a full reference if you are absolutely new to Hyper-V.

Conventions

In this book, you will find a number of styles of text that distinguish between different kinds of information. Here are some examples of these styles, and an explanation of their meaning.

Code words in text, database table names, folder names, filenames, file extensions, pathnames, dummy URLs, user input, and Twitter handles are shown as follows: "After adding these Hyper-V components, the creation of our `unattended.xml` file is completed."

A block of code is set as follows:

```
<?xml version="1.0" encoding="UTF-8"?>
<component xmlns:wcm="http://schemas.microsoft.com/WMIConfig/2002/
State" xmlns:xsi="http://www.w3.org/2001/XMLSchema-instance"
language="neutral" versionScope="nonSxS" publicKeyToken="31bf3856
ad364e35" processorArchitecture="amd64" name="Microsoft-Windows-
International-Core-WinPE">
```

```
<SetupUILanguage>
  <UILanguage>en-US</UILanguage>
</SetupUILanguage>
<InputLocale>en-US</InputLocale>
<UILanguage>en-US</UILanguage>
<SystemLocale>en-US</SystemLocale>
<UserLocale>en-US</UserLocale>
</component>
```

Any command-line input or output is written as follows:

```
Set-VMHOST -computername localhost -virtualharddiskpath 'D:\VMs'
Set-VMHOST -computername localhost -virtualmachinepath 'D:\VMs'
```

New terms and **important words** are shown in bold. Words that you see on the screen, in menus or dialog boxes for example, appear in the text like this: "Don't worry about entering a password into **Windows System Image Manager**; it will encrypt the password while saving the file."

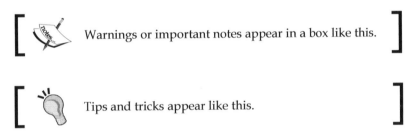

Warnings or important notes appear in a box like this.

Tips and tricks appear like this.

Reader feedback

Feedback from our readers is always welcome. Let us know what you think about this book—what you liked or may have disliked. Reader feedback is important for us to develop titles that you really get the most out of.

To send us general feedback, simply send an e-mail to feedback@packtpub.com, and mention the book title through the subject of your message.

If there is a topic that you have expertise in and you are interested in either writing or contributing to a book, see our author guide on www.packtpub.com/authors.

Customer support

Now that you are the proud owner of a Packt book, we have a number of things to help you to get the most from your purchase.

Downloading the example code

You can download the example code files for all Packt books you have purchased from your account at http://www.packtpub.com. If you purchased this book elsewhere, you can visit http://www.packtpub.com/support and register to have the files e-mailed directly to you.

Errata

Although we have taken every care to ensure the accuracy of our content, mistakes do happen. If you find a mistake in one of our books—maybe a mistake in the text or the code—we would be grateful if you would report this to us. By doing so, you can save other readers from frustration and help us improve subsequent versions of this book. If you find any errata, please report them by visiting http://www.packtpub.com/support, selecting your book, clicking on the **errata submission form** link, and entering the details of your errata. Once your errata are verified, your submission will be accepted and the errata will be uploaded to our website, or added to any list of existing errata, under the Errata section of that title.

Piracy

Piracy of copyright material on the Internet is an ongoing problem across all media. At Packt, we take the protection of our copyright and licenses very seriously. If you come across any illegal copies of our works, in any form, on the Internet, please provide us with the location address or website name immediately so that we can pursue a remedy.

Please contact us at copyright@packtpub.com with a link to the suspected pirated material.

We appreciate your help in protecting our authors, and our ability to bring you valuable content.

Questions

You can contact us at questions@packtpub.com if you are having a problem with any aspect of the book, and we will do our best to address it.

1

Accelerate Hyper-V Deployment

"Based on my slogan 'Keep It Smart and Simple (K.I.S.S.),' the planning phase is essential for a successful implementation of a Hyper-V environment."

Andreas Baumgarten – MVP System Center Cloud and Datacenter Management

This chapter provides an overview of how to automate the installation of the best practice Hyper-V host and its first running virtual machines. You will learn how to create unattended installations of Hyper-V with minimal effort. All the examples shown in this chapter are proven real-world best practice.

This chapter includes the following topics:

- Planning the Hyper-V host
- Unattended installation of Hyper-V through XML files
- Rapid deployment of virtual machines

Why Hyper-V projects fail

Before you start deploying your first production Hyper-V host, make sure that you have completed a detailed planning phase. I have been called in to many Hyper-V projects to assist in repairing what a "specialist" has implemented. Most of the time, I start to correct the design because the biggest failures happen there, but are only discovered later during implementation. I remember many projects where I was called in to assist with installations and configurations during the implementation phases, because these were the project phases where a real expert was needed.

Based on experience—this is wrong. Most critical to a successful design phase are two reasons: its rare existence and somebody with technological and organizational experience with Hyper-V. If you don't have this, look out for a Microsoft Partner with a Gold Competency called Management and Virtualization on Microsoft Pinpoint (`http://pinpoint.microsoft.com`) and take a quick look at the reviews done by customers for successful Hyper-V projects. If you think it's expensive to hire a professional, wait until you hire an amateur. Having an expert in on the design phase is the best way to accelerate your Hyper-V project.

Before you start your first deployment in production, make sure that you have defined the aim of the project and its smart criteria, and have done a thorough analysis of the current state. After this, you should be able to plan the necessary steps to reach the target state, including a pilot phase.

Planning your environment

Besides the organizational skill needed for a successful Hyper-V project, there are some helpful tools that can help in most cases with the technical details. How many hosts will I need for my Hyper-V setup? How many CPUs and how much RAM is needed? What bandwidth is needed on my network? To answer these questions, I commonly use the free Solution Accelerator, **Microsoft Assessment and Planning Toolkit (MAP Toolkit)** by Microsoft (downloadable at the shortlink, `http://bit.ly/1lzt2mJ`). The MAP Toolkit is shown in the following screenshot:

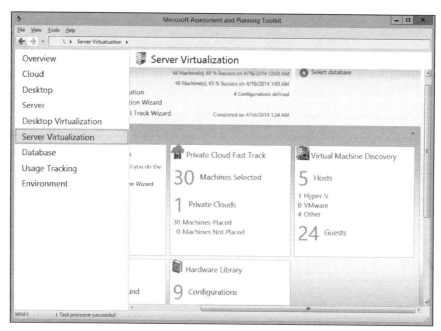

The easy-to-use MAP Toolkit does a full inventory of your existing environment, including performance counters over time. After running the wizards in your existing infrastructure, you will get an overview, a detailed report of the existing hardware and software infrastructure, and—most importantly—a measure of how these are used in your data center as of today, including used CPU cycles, memory, Storage I/O, and network usage. MAP even includes a planning wizard to plan the hardware requirements of your future Hyper-V hosts based on your current workloads and hardware configurations.

After having a basic understanding of the current usage and future needs of your hardware, it's time to choose the appropriate servers to run Hyper-V and its virtual machines. The good news is that all major server vendors have hardware in their portfolio that performs well for this task, so choose whatever vendor you like; there is just one thing you absolutely need to make sure of. The chosen hardware should be on the Windows Server Catalog and be certified for Windows Server 2012 R2 (shortlink `http://bit.ly/1gII6h7`). This way, you are making sure that your hardware has undergone extensive testing for Windows Server 2012 R2 with Hyper-V. You will be able to open a support call at Microsoft in case you ever run into problems using this hardware with Hyper-V. If you are going to use an older version of Hyper-V (which you should avoid, but licenses might force you to), select the corresponding host OS on the hardware catalog. Make sure that your host setup includes the necessary adapters to comply with your chosen storage (refer to *Chapter 4, Storage Best Practices*) and network designs (refer to *Chapter 5, Network Best Practices*).

Which CPU vendor you choose won't make a huge difference; just make sure that you stick to one, because mixed CPU vendors won't allow you to use live migration between Hyper-V hosts. Be sure that the chosen CPU models have support for server virtualization (Intel VT/AMD-V) and Data Execution Prevention (XD/NX) enabled. I strongly recommend that you use hyperthreading-enabled CPUs for server virtualization with active **Second Level Address Translation (SLAT)**. Both are hardware-accelerated CPU features that add more performance to Hyper-V. For best performance, make sure to buy CPU models from the newest certified Enterprise Server line of the vendor of your choice. Due to the current licensing of Windows Server 2012 R2 Datacenter and several other products, I recommend that you choose CPUs with as many cores per socket as financially reasonable. As of early 2014, the sweet spot was around eight cores per socket for ideal value for money.

To choose the right RAM for your Hyper-V hosts, make sure that it supports **Error Checking and Correction (ECC)** RAM and choose modules large enough to fit with the amount designed into your hosts. As RAM is very inexpensive these days, you should choose the bigger modules in case of any doubts to ensure growth in future.

For your storage and networking options, see the corresponding chapters of this book. However, to host the Hyper-V management partition, I strongly recommend that you use two local SSDs or HDDs in Raid1 and not share the disks with virtual machines or other data. I have experienced the best results with these local hard drives and have found some problems with remote boot scenarios due to the higher complexity of boot-from-SAN setups—which is also a possible, and supported, but not preferred scenario. You don't need high-performance disks for the OS; all I/O performance should be added to the VM storage.

Another important topic is to choose fewer bigger boxes over many small Hyper-V hosts. This enables more efficient management. However, while needing a failover resource in a cluster, a Hyper-V cluster should consist of at least three nodes; otherwise 50 percent of your hardware is reserved for failover scenarios.

Refer to *Chapter 6, Hyper-V Performance Tuning,* it includes advanced hardware sizing guidelines for performance tuning.

Preparing your host systems

Many "Prepare Your System" chapters start with telling you to update all your hardware and software components to the latest releases. This chapter doesn't make an exception to this rule. In no other technical area have I seen so many successful fixed environments due to firmware and driver updates. Windows Server with Hyper-V has undergone a very rapid development cycle with many releases in a short timeframe. Most hardware vendors released firmware and drivers with greatly shortened testing periods and were forced to release several updates due to firmware and driver updates to their products. Before you start setting up your Hyper-V host, update BIOS, RAID Controller, and the **Network Interface Card** (NIC) firmware to their latest release. Use the home page of the server-vendor, not the vendor of the individual components, for reference to the latest certified releases. Use only downloads from the individual components' vendor if you see those problems you encounter fixed by the corresponding release notes.

Other than this, you only need your Hyper-V installation media, the Windows 8.1 ADK (shortlink `http://bit.ly/1jAfero`), and a USB drive to prepare for rapid Hyper-V installations. Download either the full version of Windows Server 2012 R2 with Hyper-V from your Volume Licence Portal or the 180-day Evaluation version of Hyper-V (shortlink `http://bit.ly/1hIREXL`). In fact, it does not make any difference whether you use the Evaluation edition or the full version media—they are interchangeable—the only difference will be made by the product key you enter. All Hyper-V features are also supported by the free editions of Hyper-V Server 2012 R2 (shortlink `http://bit.ly/1oL1lbM`); all the screenshots and configurations you see in this book are created using the full version of Windows Server 2012 R2 with Hyper-V and could vary slightly from the free edition. Hyper-V is very easy to install.

To familiarize yourself with Hyper-V, just insert the installation media, select it as the boot device, and click through the various options in the setup wizard. If this will be the only Hyper-V host you will ever install, this will be a great installation experience. Most of the time, you will not stick to just one host, and to speed up things, we will mainly use unattended installations of the Hyper-V hosts from now on. The unattended setup uses configurations saved in a precreated `unattended.xml` file, which can be either slipstreamed into the installation media or saved on a USB drive so that it's available to the host during installation. This enables a standardized and very rapid Hyper-V deployment with a onetime preparation.

Creating unattended installation files

To create an `unattended.xml` file, you can either start from scratch with a simple text editor or use a GUI. To leverage the second option, start the setup of the Windows **Assessment and Deployment Kit (ADK)** you downloaded earlier. At the setup prompt, select only **Deployment Tools**, as shown in the following screenshot. After the completion of the installation, start **Windows System Image Manager** from the Start screen:

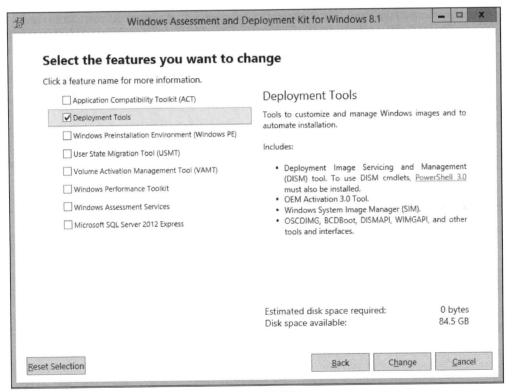

Windows ADK 8.1

After the tool is fully loaded, select the **File** menu, open the **Select an Image** wizard, and browse to the `Install.wim` file or your installation media in the source's subdirectory. Select the Windows Server 2012 R2 SERVERSTANDARD edition for your first unattended installation file and allow the creation of a new catalog file. If you receive a warning message stating that you are unable to write the catalog file, open Windows Explorer, navigate to the `Install.wim` file, open its properties, and uncheck the **read only** checkbox. If you have your installation media sitting on a physical read-only media, copy `Install.wim` to a local hard drive first. Select the Server Standard Edition with GUI:

Select Windows Edition

After the catalog creation is completed, select the **File** menu again, create a **New Answer File**, and save it as `unattended.xml` to a place of your choice.

Windows System Image Manager will then create the basic XML structure of your unattended file, as shown in the following screenshot:

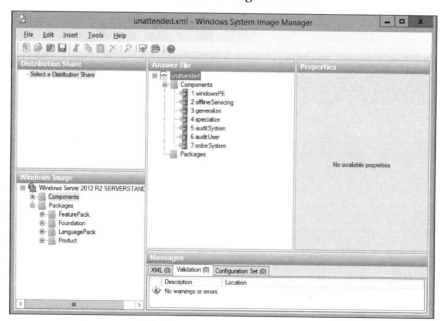

Windows System Image Manager

Opening this XML file in Internet Explorer will show you the actual file contents. Every Windows Server 2012 R2 setup will check for an existing `unattended.xml` file at the start of every available drive letter, but will only work if the XML structure is correct. We will now continue to fill this `unattended.xml` file with contents specific to the Hyper-V setup to allow a Zero-Touch installation of your Hyper-V hosts.

Adding basic components

Start by adding the most basic components by expanding the **Components** tree under the **Windows Image** section in the left-hand side corner of the tool. Let's now add language and locale information:

1. First, add the `amd64_Microsoft-Windows-International-Core-WinPE` components to `Pass1` and fill it with the basic language options. The generated XML part with all the mandatory parameters will look like the following code:

   ```
   <?xml version="1.0" encoding="UTF-8"?>
   <component xmlns:wcm="http://schemas.microsoft.com/WMIConfig/2002/
   State" xmlns:xsi="http://www.w3.org/2001/XMLSchema-instance"
   language="neutral" versionScope="nonSxS" publicKeyToken="31bf3856
   ad364e35" processorArchitecture="amd64" name="Microsoft-Windows-
   International-Core-WinPE">
     <SetupUILanguage>
       <UILanguage>en-US</UILanguage>
     </SetupUILanguage>
     <InputLocale>en-US</InputLocale>
     <UILanguage>en-US</UILanguage>
     <SystemLocale>en-US</SystemLocale>
     <UserLocale>en-US</UserLocale>
   </component>
   ```

   If you prefer language settings other than US English, make sure that the language components are included in the installation media and refer to the correct locale IDs, which can be found on Microsoft MSDN (shortlink `http://bit.ly/1gMNu2B`).

2. Next, add `amd64_Microsoft-Windows-Setup_neutral` to `Pass1` to configure some basic OS configurations such as Disk Layout. A generated sample XML part for a BIOS-based system is as follows:

   ```
   <?xml version="1.0" encoding="UTF-8"?>
   <component xmlns:wcm="http://schemas.microsoft.com/WMIConfig/2002/
   State" xmlns:xsi="http://www.w3.org/2001/XMLSchema-instance"
   language="neutral" versionScope="nonSxS" publicKeyToken="31bf3856
   ad364e35" processorArchitecture="amd64" name="Microsoft-Windows-
   Setup">
   ```

```xml
<DiskConfiguration>
  <Disk wcm:action="add">
    <CreatePartitions>
      <CreatePartition wcm:action="add">
        <Order>1</Order>
        <Size>350</Size>
        <Type>Primary</Type>
      </CreatePartition>
      <CreatePartition wcm:action="add">
        <Order>2</Order>
        <Extend>true</Extend>
        <Type>Primary</Type>
      </CreatePartition>
    </CreatePartitions>
    <ModifyPartitions>
      <ModifyPartition wcm:action="add">
        <Active>true</Active>
        <Format>NTFS</Format>
        <Label>Bitlocker</Label>
        <Order>1</Order>
        <PartitionID>1</PartitionID>
      </ModifyPartition>
      <ModifyPartition wcm:action="add">
        <Letter>C</Letter>
        <Label>HostOS</Label>
        <Order>2</Order>
        <PartitionID>2</PartitionID>
      </ModifyPartition>
    </ModifyPartitions>
    <DiskID>0</DiskID>
    <WillWipeDisk>true</WillWipeDisk>
  </Disk>
</DiskConfiguration>
</component>
```

This configuration will make sure that there are clean partitions that follow Microsoft's default deployment model. The small partition at the start of the disk is created to support Bitlocker. Microsoft's full disk encryption can be used with Hyper-V hosts and can also be activated later. The use of Bitlocker is only recommended in high-security environments.

3. If your host does not have BIOS anymore and uses an UEFI-based setup routine, the XML file will be edited to include the following code as well:

```
<?xml version="1.0" encoding="UTF-8"?>
<component xmlns:wcm="http://schemas.microsoft.com/WMIConfig/2002/
State" xmlns:xsi="http://www.w3.org/2001/XMLSchema-instance"
language="neutral" versionScope="nonSxS" publicKeyToken="31bf3856
ad364e35" processorArchitecture="amd64" name="Microsoft-Windows-
Setup">
  <DiskConfiguration>
    <Disk wcm:action="add">
      <CreatePartitions>
        <CreatePartition wcm:action="add">
          <Order>2</Order>
          <Size>100</Size>
          <Type>EFI</Type>
        </CreatePartition>
        <CreatePartition wcm:action="add">
          <Order>3</Order>
          <Extend>false</Extend>
          <Type>MSR</Type>
          <Size>128</Size>
        </CreatePartition>
        <CreatePartition wcm:action="add">
          <Order>4</Order>
          <Extend>true</Extend>
          <Type>Primary</Type>
        </CreatePartition>
        <CreatePartition wcm:action="add">
          <Size>350</Size>
          <Type>Primary</Type>
          <Order>1</Order>
        </CreatePartition>
      </CreatePartitions>
      <ModifyPartitions>
        <ModifyPartition wcm:action="add">
          <Active>false</Active>
          <Format>NTFS</Format>
          <Label>Bitlocker</Label>
          <Order>1</Order>
          <PartitionID>1</PartitionID>
        </ModifyPartition>
        <ModifyPartition wcm:action="add">
```

```
          <Letter>C</Letter>
          <Label>HostOS</Label>
          <Order>3</Order>
          <PartitionID>3</PartitionID>
          <Format>NTFS</Format>
        </ModifyPartition>
        <ModifyPartition wcm:action="add">
          <Order>2</Order>
          <PartitionID>2</PartitionID>
          <Label>EFI</Label>
          <Format>FAT32</Format>
          <Active>false</Active>
        </ModifyPartition>
      </ModifyPartitions>
      <DiskID>0</DiskID>
      <WillWipeDisk>true</WillWipeDisk>
    </Disk>
  </DiskConfiguration>
</component>
```

Which edition to install

In the earlier versions of Windows Server with Hyper-V, there were huge differences among the different available editions. Some features and hardware requirements were only available on Enterprise and Datacenter editions of Windows Server. Almost all the features and hardware specifications are available even with the Standard edition of Windows Server 2012 R2, so there is no need to use an Enterprise edition (which was dropped by Microsoft earlier). The main difference between the Standard and Datacenter editions relies on the virtualization rights. Each Windows Server Standard edition allows you to run two guest **Operating System Environments (OSEs)** with Windows Server editions, and a Datacenter edition allows you to run an unlimited number of Windows Server VMs on this particular licensed Hyper-V host. There is only one technical difference between the two editions: on a Datacenter edition, all Windows Server guest VMs will be automatically activated, when provided with a corresponding key during setup. There is no need for a MAK or KMS-based OS activation anymore.

Basically, it's not very important which edition you choose for the host install, so stick to Windows Server 2012 R2 Standard. If you want to leverage **Automatic Virtual Machine Activation (AVMA)**, install a Datacenter edition on the host. It is easy to upgrade a Standard edition later to a Datacenter edition, but there is no downgrade option.

If you are not sure which edition you are using, open a PowerShell window with administrative privileges and run the following command:

```
get-windowsedition -online
```

To find out which editions are available for upgrade, run the following command:

```
Get-WindowsEdition -online -target
```

Finally, to upgrade to the target edition, run the following command:

```
Set-WindowsEdition -online -edition ServerDatacenter
```

While it's suitable to install a Datacenter edition on a Hyper-V host, you should never do this inside a virtual machine. Installing Standard editions into virtual machines always gives you an easy way to move this VM at a later time to a non-Datacenter Hyper-V host.

The next step to build our unattended installation is to set up the installation target and edition. Navigate to the `ImageInstall` string under the `Microsoft-Windows-Setup` node and add the following code:

```
<ImageInstall><OSImage><InstallFrom><MetaData wcm:action="add"><Key>/
Image/Name</Key><Value>Windows Server 2012 R2 SERVERSTANDARD</Value></
MetaData></InstallFrom><InstallTo><DiskID>0</DiskID><PartitionID>2</
PartitionID></InstallTo></OSImage></ImageInstall>
```

If you have chosen the UEFI-based setup, choose `PartitionID 4` according to your disk setup. This will make sure that you install the Standard edition of Windows Server 2012 R2 to the correct partition.

As the last step in `Pass1`, we will fill out the `UserData` tree under the `Microsoft-Windows-Setup` node and edit the following code:

```
<UserData><ProductKey><WillShowUI>OnError</WillShowUI></
ProductKey><AcceptEula>true</AcceptEula><FullName>YourName</
FullName><Organization>YourOrg</Organization></UserData>
```

Fill in **Name** and **Org Data** with anything you like; however, these fields are mandatory. The **product key** field is optional. If you intend to use a 180-day trial version of Windows Server or are leveraging KMS Server activation capabilities, do not enter a product key. If you are using MAK-based OS activations, enter your product key. You can also install a MAK product key at a later time by opening a PowerShell window with administrative privileges and running the following command:

```
slmgr -upk (this uninstalls the current product key) and
slmgr -ipk <key> (including dashes)
```

To GUI or not to GUI

After adding the basic parameters, it's now time to add some comfort to our Zero-Touch installation.

In **Windows System Image Manager,** add amd64_Microsoft-Windows-Shell-Setup_neutral to Pass4 and Pass7.

Edit the XML file to set your time zone settings (run tzutil /l in a Shell to get a list of all the valid time zones) and your local administrator password. Don't worry about entering a password into **Windows System Image Manager**; it will encrypt the password while saving the file. The following code shows how to set the regional and user information:

```
<settings pass="specialize"><component language="neutral"
xmlns:xsi="http://www.w3.org/2001/XMLSchema-instance"
xmlns:wcm="http://schemas.microsoft.com/WMIConfig/2002/State"
versionScope="nonSxS" publicKeyToken="31bf3856ad364e35"
processorArchitecture="amd64" name="Microsoft-Windows-Shell-
Setup"><TimeZone>W. Europe Standard Time</TimeZone></component>
</settings><settings pass="oobeSystem"><component language="neutral"
xmlns:xsi="http://www.w3.org/2001/XMLSchema-instance"
xmlns:wcm="http://schemas.microsoft.com/WMIConfig/2002/
State" versionScope="nonSxS" publicKeyToken="31bf3856ad364e35"
processorArchitecture="amd64" name="Microsoft-Windows-Shell-Setup
"><UserAccounts><AdministratorPassword><Value>UABAAHMAcwB3ADAAcg
BkAEEAZABtAGkAbgBpAHMAdAByAGEAdABvAHIAUABhAHMAcwB3AG8AcgBkAA==</
Value><PlainText>false</PlainText></AdministratorPassword></
UserAccounts></component></settings>
```

To allow a rapid deployment of hosts, I have not entered a computer name at this stage, so the setup will generate a random computer name for each node installed. If you want to enter a computer name, add the following code to your XML-specialized section:

```
<ComputerName>Hyper-V01</ComputerName>
```

Another optional feature was selected right at the beginning of our XML creation: the GUI. By selecting the Windows Server Standard edition and not the Standard Core edition, we have included the complete GUI of Windows Server in our setup. Unlike previous versions of Windows Server with Hyper-V, the GUI is now a feature that can be activated and deactivated at a later stage. Please note that the GUI is not available on the free Hyper-V Server 2012 R2. The full GUI installation process offers the same great user experience we know for many versions of Windows Server and Windows Client operating systems, but Server Core is the recommended installation method by Microsoft for Windows Server 2012 R2 and Hyper-V. The Core installation option offers a reduced attack surface with less patching efforts and fewer reboots. It even comes with a smaller resource footprint than its Full GUI equivalent. However, offering only a PowerShell Window as the single point of local administration discouraged many system administrators in the past, so Core setups aren't found often. Don't forget that all administrative APIs are active on a Core Server, so you can connect with your MMC consoles from other servers or clients without the need to use the PowerShell modules. With Windows Server 2012 R2, you have even more choices; Microsoft added the MinShell installation mode where, in addition to PowerShell, all administrative consoles, known from the **Remote Server Administrations Tools (RSAT)**, are available locally, but security critical elements such as Internet Explorer still aren't presented locally. Following customer feedback, MinShell is getting more attention than the older Core setup. Both Core and MinShell do offer another huge advantage: they don't allow the installation of programs and configurations that require a GUI, though these systems are typically very clean in terms of software onboard, adding to a seamless operation in a production environment. The following best practice model was established by our customers to manage the GUI:

1. Install the Server with Full GUI. Make yourself familiar with the operating system and its roles.

2. After finishing the initial configuration, uninstall the GUI and run the server in the MinShell or Core mode.

3. To switch from Full Server GUI to Minshell later on, open a PowerShell Window with administrative privileges and run `Uninstall-WindowsFeature Server-Gui-Shell –Restart` for MinShell and `Get-WindowsFeature *gui* | Uninstall-WindowsFeature –Restart` for Server Core.

4. To reinstall MinShell, run the following command:

```
Install-WindowsFeature Server-Gui-Mgmt-Infra -Restart
```

5. To reinstall Full Server GUI, run the following command:

```
Install-WindowsFeature Server-Gui-Mgmt-Infra, Server-Gui-Shell
-Restart
```

In every case, a reboot of the host will occur. Look at the Windows Server Core PowerShell shown in the following screenshot:

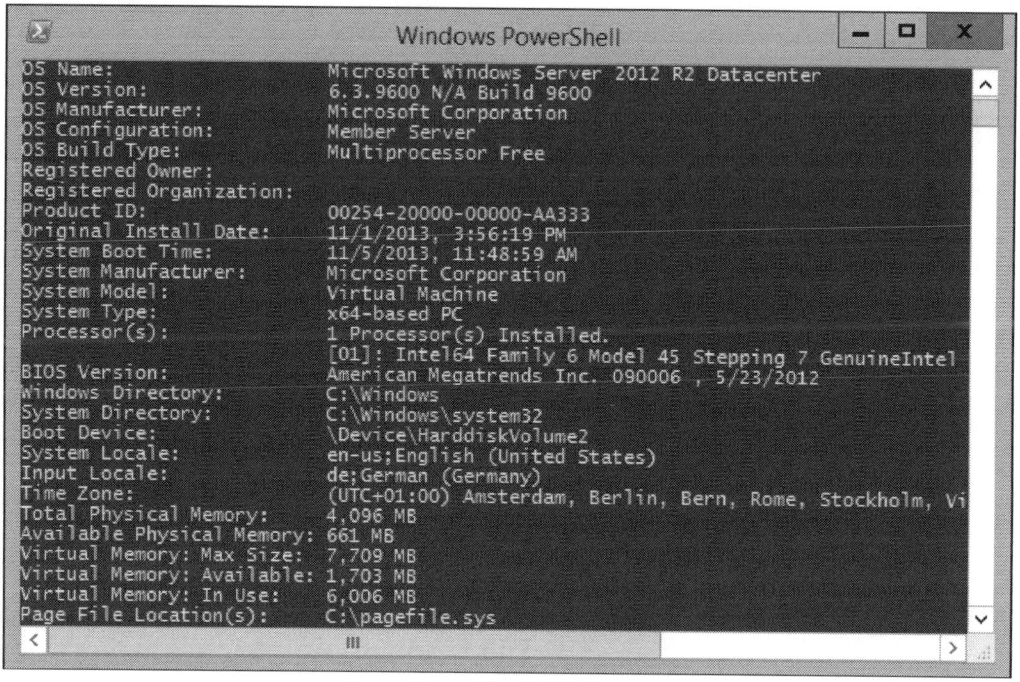

Server Core without GUI elements

Hyper-V hosts in Active Directory domains

The basic operating system setup will now already be based on a Zero-Touch installation, but we want to achieve more than this and will include some additional options.

Add the amd64_Microsoft-Windows-TerminalServices-LocalSessionManager component to Pass4 and configure it to enable Remote Desktop Access to the server:

```
<?xml version="1.0" encoding="UTF-8"?>
<component xmlns:wcm="http://schemas.microsoft.com/WMIConfig/2002/
State" xmlns:xsi="http://www.w3.org/2001/XMLSchema-instance"
language="neutral" versionScope="nonSxS" publicKeyToken="31bf3856
ad364e35" processorArchitecture="amd64" name="Microsoft-Windows-
TerminalServices-LocalSessionManager">
  <fDenyTSConnections>false</fDenyTSConnections>
</component>
```

To reach the Server via RDP via its designated IP address, we will also set the basic network settings. Keep in mind that based on your converged network setup for Hyper-V, these might be overwritten at a later step (*Chapter 5, Network Best Practices*).

Add the amd64_Microsoft-Windows-TCPIP component to Pass4 and configure a static IP Address—in this case, based on the name of the interface. This is also possible using the MAC address. Configure the network as shown in the following code:

```
<?xml version="1.0" encoding="UTF-8"?>
<component xmlns:wcm="http://schemas.microsoft.com/WMIConfig/2002/
State" xmlns:xsi="http://www.w3.org/2001/XMLSchema-instance"
language="neutral" versionScope="nonSxS" publicKeyToken="31bf3856ad36
4e35" processorArchitecture="amd64" name="Microsoft-Windows-TCPIP">
  <Interfaces>
    <Interface wcm:action="add">
      <Ipv4Settings>
        <DhcpEnabled>false</DhcpEnabled>
        <Metric>10</Metric>
        <RouterDiscoveryEnabled>true</RouterDiscoveryEnabled>
      </Ipv4Settings>
      <UnicastIpAddresses>
        <IpAddress wcm:action="add" wcm:keyValue="1">192.168.1.41/24</
IpAddress>
      </UnicastIpAddresses>
      <Identifier>Local Area Connection</Identifier>
    </Interface>
  </Interfaces>
</component>
```

Whether Hyper-V hosts should be added to an Active Directory domain is a topic that is often discussed. Having seen a lot of Hyper-V environments, either domain-joined or workgroup-joined, my answer to this is a strong yes. Windows Server 2012 R2 Servers can boot up even clusters when domain-joined without an Active Directory domain controller available, so this chicken-or-egg problem from earlier Hyper-V versions is not a problem any more. Hyper-V will run without an Active Directory domain; however, very basic capabilities such as live migration won't be available on workgroup environments. Huge Hyper-V installations or high-security companies even leverage their own management domain to place their Hyper-V hosts into an Active Directory domain.

There is little security consideration standing against a huge management benefit, through credential management, group policies, and so on, so you should domain-join all Hyper-V hosts to your existing Active Directory domain. If your Hyper-V hosts will be placed in high-security environments, join them to a dedicated management domain (within a separated Active Directory forest) and not to your production domain.

Add the `amd64_Microsoft-Windows-UnattendedJoin` component to `Pass4` and configure it to join an existing Active Directory domain:

```xml
<?xml version="1.0" encoding="UTF-8"?>
<component xmlns:wcm="http://schemas.microsoft.com/WMIConfig/2002/
State" xmlns:xsi="http://www.w3.org/2001/XMLSchema-instance"
language="neutral" versionScope="nonSxS" publicKeyToken="31bf3856
ad364e35" processorArchitecture="amd64" name="Microsoft-Windows-
UnattendedJoin">
  <Identification>
    <Credentials>
      <Domain>Elanity.local</Domain>
      <Password>Hannover96</Password>
      <Username>joindomain</Username>
    </Credentials>
    <JoinDomain>Elanity.de</JoinDomain>
    <MachineObjectOU>OU=Hyper-V,DC=Elanity,DC=local</MachineObjectOU>
  </Identification>
</component>
```

A typical configuration that is seen in this step is the disabling of the Windows Firewall. In my opinion, this is a bad practice. The Windows Firewall is a great layer of security and should be configured to your needs, but not disabled. For a central Firewall configuration, we'll use Group Policy settings, so we don't need to include any configuration in our `unattended.xml`.

Activating Hyper-V features

After our operating system is prepared to host Hyper-V, it's time to activate the Hyper-V components. Add the following product packages and their roles and features to your `unattended.xml` file:

```xml
<?xml version="1.0" encoding="UTF-8"?>
<servicing>
  <package action="configure">
    <assemblyIdentity language="" publicKeyToken="31bf3856ad3
64e35" processorArchitecture="amd64" name="Microsoft-Windows-
ServerStandardEdition" version="6.3.9600.16384" />
    <selection name="Microsoft-Hyper-V-Common-Drivers-Package"
state="true" />
    <selection name="Microsoft-Hyper-V-Guest-Integration-Drivers-
Package" state="true" />
    <selection name="Microsoft-Hyper-V-Server-Drivers-Package"
state="true" />
    <selection name="Microsoft-Hyper-V-ServerEdition-Package"
state="true" />
  </package>
  <package action="configure">
    <assemblyIdentity language="" publicKeyToken="31bf3856ad364e35"
processorArchitecture="amd64" name="Microsoft-Windows-ServerCore-
Package" version="6.3.9600.16384" />
    <selection name="Microsoft-Hyper-V" state="true" />
    <selection name="Microsoft-Hyper-V-Offline" state="true" />
    <selection name="Microsoft-Hyper-V-Online" state="true" />
    <selection name="VmHostAgent" state="true" />
    <selection name="AdminUI" state="true" />
    <selection name="ServerManager-Core-RSAT" state="true" />
    <selection name="ServerManager-Core-RSAT-Feature-Tools"
state="true" />
    <selection name="ServerManager-Core-RSAT-Role-Tools" state="true"
/>
  </package>
</servicing>
```

After adding these Hyper-V components, the creation of our `unattended.xml` file is completed. You can download the complete sample XML file (`http://bit.ly/1xBIQb2`). Place the file in the root folder on the USB drive and boot the Server system from your installation media. You will now experience a fully Zero-Touch Hyper-V installation. In *Chapter 2, High Availability Scenarios*, you will learn how to advance this even further into a Zero-Touch cluster installation.

Unattended.XML file for automatic Hyper-V setup

Post-installation tasks

Be sure to remove the USB drive with the unattended setup file prior to moving the host to production. A host reboot could otherwise force a reinstallation, including a wipe of all hard drives, due to the trigger of another unattended installation.

Run Windows Update to make sure that you have installed all the available updates. Are there any Windows updates you should not install on Hyper-V hosts? Yes, drivers should not be installed over a Windows Update unless support tells you to do so. However, besides this, install every available Windows update in all of your Hyper-V hosts. Check out the update list for Hyper-V to check whether there are any Hotfixes available that are recommended for installation but not yet available through Windows Update (shortlink `http://bit.ly/1kx0yYS`).

The Hyper-V role is already enabled, and we are ready to create virtual machines. To ensure network connectivity and safe operations of our VMs, we will configure some additional parameters after the installation.

First of all, we need some basic network connectivity for our virtual machines. If you have a second **Network Interface Card (NIC)** available in your host, run the following command in an elevated PowerShell session:

```
New-VMSwitch -Name external -NetAdapterName "Local Area Connection 2"
```

If you have only one NIC, run the following command:

```
New-VMSwitch -Name external -NetAdapterName "Local Area Connection"
-AllowManagementOS $true
```

Now, your virtual machines can use an external Hyper-V switch named "external" to communicate over the network.

Ever wondered about the many errors your RDP-mapped printer can create on a Hyper-V host? I could not believe this for a long time, but recently, I have seen a blue-screened Hyper-V Server due to improper printing drivers. Do you need to print from a Hyper-V host? Absolutely not! So, make sure that you disable RDP Printer Mapping through a Group Policy (or Local Policy).

Navigate to **Computer Configuration | Policies | Administrative Templates | Windows Components | Remote Desktop Services | Remote Desktop Session Host | Printer Redirection | Do not allow client printer redirection | Enable** in a Group Policy.

Hyper-V uses some default paths to store virtual machine configuration and its hard disks. I find this very interesting but definitely not suitable for a production environment. Make sure that you change the default paths, if possible to a non-system drive, by running the following commands in an elevated PowerShell window:

```
Set-VMHOST -computername localhost -virtualharddiskpath 'D:\VMs'

Set-VMHOST -computername localhost -virtualmachinepath 'D:\VMs'
```

I have not seen any issues with placing VM configuration files and virtual hard disks into the same folder structure. You have everything your VM configuration depends on in one place.

Another important post-installation task is to follow the rule: do not install other roles on Hyper-V hosts. A Hyper-V host is a Hyper-V host and nothing else. Move all the other services into virtual machines that run on the Hyper-V host.

Moreover, also keep the following points in mind:

- Do not install any features other than Failover Clustering and **Multipath I/O (MPIO)** on a Hyper-V host

    There are exceptions in an SMB3 scenario where you also want to install **Datacenter Bridging (DCB)** and SMB bandwidth limits

- Limit software installations to an absolute minimum, that is, backup and monitoring agents

Antivirus on a Hyper-V host

Another great topic for discussion is whether you should install an antivirus client on a Hyper-V host or not. Many companies have compliance rules stating that on every Server or every Windows machine, an AV client needs to be installed. If there is a rule like this in place, follow it and install an AV agent on your Hyper-V hosts. Make sure that you also implement the long list of files, which contain all the Hyper-V configuration files and virtual machine data, you have to exclude from your scans.

I have seen antivirus engines on Hyper-V hosts doing bad things such as breaking a virtual hard disk, deleting an essential system file, or just producing a very intense amount of storage IOs. Excluding all relevant files and folders regarding Hyper-V and its VMs, there is nothing left worth scanning on a Hyper-V host. If you are not bound by a compliance policy, I highly recommend that you do not install antivirus products on Hyper-V.

There are some approaches for Hyper-V-aware antivirus products; however, I have not seen one flawless working solution as of today, so you should protect your VMs from malware from inside the VM by installing your AV agents into the virtual machines.

Setting the Pagefile

One of the most frequent configuration tips around Hyper-V hosts is to manually configure the Pagefile. The values described are sometimes quite creative.

After doing many tests with Hyper-V hosts with all different kinds of RAM configurations and deep technology-oriented exchanges with Microsoft Product Teams, including the Hyper-V Product Team itself, on how Pagefile management is working in Windows Server 2012 R2, there is only one recommendation I have today: leave it alone.

The Windows Pagefile is by default managed by Windows. If you have followed all other best practices described up to this point and, most importantly, you did ___ (management OS), you are all ___ a better efficiency in PageFile ___ configuration. I have not seen a ___ 2 R2 as of now that had problems

___ he Pagefile configuration of the

___ s for performance management ___ manage the Pagefile as shown in

Pagefile configuration

Creating virtual machines

You are all set, and it's time to create some virtual machines. To do a rapid deployment of virtual machines, we will rely on PowerShell.

Creating a new virtual machine with PowerShell is easy; just open an elevated PowerShell prompt, and run the following command:

```
New-VM
```

Without any additional parameters, this will create a new virtual machine with the default parameters. To create a new Generation 2 VM, run the following command:

```
New-VM –Generation 2
```

To create a new virtual machine with a specified name, a custom path to store the VM files, and a memory configuration, run the following command:

```
New-VM –Name VM01 –Path C:\VM01 –Memorystartupbytes 1024MB
```

Your newly created virtual machine doesn't have a hard disk yet. Create a new VHDX file by running the following command:

```
New-VHD -Path C:\vms\vm01\vm01_c.vhdx -SizeBytes 60GB -Dynamic
```

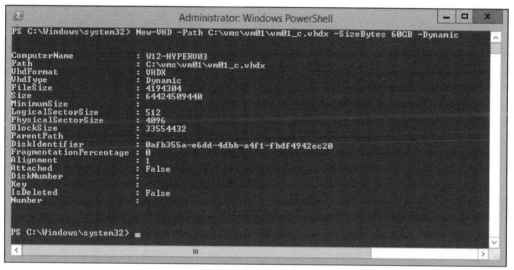

The new VHD cmdlet

The created VHDX is not yet attached to a virtual machine. Do this by running the following command:

```
Add-VMHardDiskDrive -VMName VM01 -Path C:\vms\vm01\vm01_c.vhdx
```

To add a network adapter to our virtual machine, run the following command:

```
Add-VMNetworkAdapter -vmname "VM01" -switchname "external"
```

Then, start the VM by running the following command:

```
Start-VM –Name VM01
```

You will recognize that the virtual machine now has all the basic hardware parameters but fails to boot due to a missing operating system. There are multiple ways to create an operating system for a standard VM. The most granular way to achieve this is using Virtual Machine Manager templates (see *Chapter 7, Management with System Center,* for details), but there are great capabilities already included in Windows Server 2012 R2. The approach that is seen most often is to manually install the first virtual machine and include everything you want in each of your virtual machines, such as operating system, updates, and backup agents. Then, sysprep the virtual machine by executing `sysprep.exe` present at `C:\Windows\System32\sysprep\` with the **Generalize** and **OOBE** options and shut down the virtual machine. Copy it to a template folder and mark this as read only. With Windows Server 2012 R2, you can even copy and export running virtual machines.

If you need a new virtual machine, just copy the `Template` folder, rename it to your machine name, and a preinstalled operating system with all your previous created configurations are still available. If you even want to save this first manual installation, there is a free tool for you. In Microsoft's TechNet Gallery, you will find a tool called Convert-WindowsImage that creates a fully functional VHDX template just from the operating system's installation media for you (download it from the shortlink at `http://bit.ly/1odCElX`):

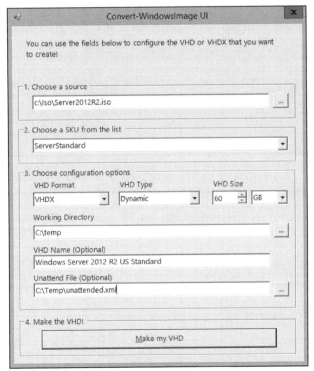

Convert-WindowsImage UI

It is even possible to run your `unattended.xml` file created with Windows System Image Manager directly through this tool, out of the box.

If you don't like patching all your images and archived VMs manually, you can use a solution to update these VHD/VHDx files offline with Apply-WindowsUpdate. ps1—just another Gem from the TechNet Gallery (download this from the shortlink at `http://bit.ly/1o4sczI`).

As you have seen in this chapter, I have mainly used Generation 2 VMs. If your guest operating systems are Windows Server 2012 and higher, this should be your default option. Generation 2 VMs allow faster booting, better stability, and smaller attack surface through a greatly reduced set of legacy hardware.

Summary

With the tools from this chapter and the configuration files you have already created up to now, you will be able to deploy new Hyper-V hosts and VMs faster and in a more reliable way than ever before. Besides this, you learned valuable best practices to plan and configure your single Hyper-V host. Continue with *Chapter 2, High Availability Scenarios*, to create high-available solutions based on your current setup to leverage additional capabilities of Hyper-V and virtualization.

2

High Availability Scenarios

"Live Migration between hosts in a Hyper-V cluster is very straightforward and requires no specific configuration, apart from type and amount of simultaneous Live Migrations. If you add multiple clusters and standalone Hyper-V hosts into the mix, I strongly advise you to configure Kerberos Constrained Delegation for all hosts and clusters involved."

Hans Vredevoort – MVP Hyper-V

This chapter will guide you through the installation of Hyper-V clusters and their best practice configuration. After installing the first Hyper-V host, it may be necessary to add another layer of availability to your virtualization services. With Failover Clusters, you get independence from hardware failures and are protected from planned or unplanned service outages.

This chapter includes the following topics:

- Prerequirements and implementation of Failover Clusters
- Cluster and quorum configuration
- Live Migration and Live Migration protocols
- Guest clustering and shared VHDX files

Preparing for High Availability

Like every project, a **High Availability (HA)** scenario starts with a planning phase. Virtualization projects are often turning up the question for additional availability for the first time in an environment. In traditional data centers with physical server systems and local storage systems, an outage of a hardware component will only affect one server hosting one service. The source of the outage can be localized very fast and the affected parts can be replaced in a short amount of time. Server virtualization comes with great benefits, such as improved operating efficiency and reduced hardware dependencies. However, a single component failure can impact a lot of virtualized systems at once. By adding redundant systems, these single points of failure can be avoided.

Planning a HA environment

The most important factor in the decision whether you need a HA environment is your business requirements. You need to find out how often and how long an IT-related production service can be interrupted, unplanned, or planned, without causing a serious problem to your business. Those requirements are defined in a central IT strategy of a business as well as in process definitions that are IT-driven. They include Service Level Agreements of critical business services run in the various departments of your company. If those definitions do not exist or are unavailable, talk to the process owners to find out the level of availability needed. High Availability is structured in different classes, measured by the total uptime in a defined timespan, that is 99.999 percent in a year. Every nine in this figure adds a huge amount of complexity and money needed to ensure this availability, so take time to find out the real availability needed by your services and resist the temptation to plan running every service on multi-redundant, geo-spread cluster systems, as it may not fit in the budget.

Be sure to plan for additional capacity in a HA environment, so you can lose hardware components without the need to sacrifice application performance.

Overview of the Failover Cluster

A Hyper-V Failover Cluster consists of two or more Hyper-V Server compute nodes. Technically, it's possible to use a Failover Cluster with just one computing node; however, it will not provide any availability advantages over a standalone host and is typically only used for migration scenarios. A Failover Cluster is hosting roles such as Hyper-V virtual machines on its computing nodes. If one node fails due to a hardware problem, it will not answer any more to cluster heartbeat communication, even though the service interruption is almost instantly detected. The virtual machines running on the particular node are powered off immediately due to the hardware failure on their computing node. The remaining cluster nodes then immediately take over these VMs in an unplanned failover process and start them on their respective own hardware. The virtual machines will be the backup running after a successful boot of their operating systems and applications in just a few minutes. Hyper-V Failover Clusters work under the condition that all compute nodes have access to a shared storage instance, holding the virtual machine configuration data and its virtual hard disks. In case of a planned failover, that is, for patching compute nodes, it's possible to move running virtual machines from one cluster node to another without interrupting the VM. All cluster nodes can run virtual machines at the same time, as long as there is enough failover capacity running all services when a node goes down. Even though a Hyper-V cluster is still called a Failover Cluster—utilizing the Windows Server Failover-Clustering feature—it is indeed capable of running an Active/Active Cluster.

To ensure that all these capabilities of a Failover Cluster are indeed working, it demands an accurate planning and implementation process.

Failover Cluster prerequirements

To successfully implement a Hyper-V Failover Cluster, we need suitable hardware, software, permissions, and network and storage infrastructure as outlined in the following sections.

Hardware

The hardware used in a Failover Cluster environment needs to be validated against the Windows Server Catalogue, as we did in *Chapter 1, Accelerate Hyper-V Deployment*. Microsoft will only support Hyper-V clusters when all components are certified for Windows Server 2012 R2.

The servers used to run our HA virtual machines should ideally consist of identical hardware models with identical components. It is possible, and supported, to run servers in the same cluster with different hardware components, that is, different size of RAM; however, due to a higher level of complexity, this is not best practice.

Special planning considerations are needed to address the CPU requirements of a cluster. To ensure maximum compatibility, all CPUs in a cluster should be exactly the same model. While it's possible from a technical point of view to mix even CPUs from Intel and AMD in the same cluster through to different architecture, you will lose core cluster capabilities such as Live Migration.

Choosing a single vendor for your CPUs is not enough, even when using different CPU models your cluster nodes may be using a different set of CPU instruction set extensions. With different instructions sets, Live Migrations won't work either. There is a compatibility mode that disables most of the instruction set on all CPUs on all cluster nodes; however, this leaves you with a negative impact on performance and should be avoided. A better approach to this problem would be creating another cluster from the legacy CPUs running smaller or non-production workloads without affecting your high-performance production workloads.

If you want to extend your cluster after some time, you will find yourself with the problem of not having the exact same hardware available to purchase. Choose the current revision of the model or product line you are already using in your cluster and manually compare the CPU instruction sets at `http://ark.intel.com/` and `http://products.amd.com/`, respectively. Choose the current CPU model that best fits the original CPU features of your cluster and have this design validated by your hardware partner.

Ensure that your servers are equipped with compatible CPUs, the same amount of RAM, and the same network cards and storage controllers.

The network design

Mixing different vendors of network cards in a single server is fine and best practice for availability, but make sure all your Hyper-V hosts are using an identical hardware setup. A network adapter should only be used exclusively for LAN traffic or storage traffic. Do not mix these two types of communication in any basic scenario. There are some more advanced scenarios involving converged networking that can enable mixed traffic, but in most cases, this is a not good idea. A Hyper-V Failover Cluster requires multiple layers of communication between its nodes and storage systems. Hyper-V networking and storage options have changed dramatically through the different releases of Hyper-V. With Windows Server 2012 R2, the network design options are endless; see *Chapter 5*, *Network Best Practices*, for details. In this chapter, we will work with a typically seen basic set of network designs. We have at least six **Network Interface Cards** (**NICs**) available in our servers with a bandwidth of 1 Gb/s. If you have more than five interface cards available per server, use NIC Teaming to ensure the availability of the network, or even use converged networking (both features are also introduced in *Chapter 5*, *Network Best Practices*). Converged networking will also be your choice if you have less than five network adapters available.

1. The First NIC will be exclusively used for Host Communication to our Hyper-V host and will not be involved in the VM network traffic or cluster communication at any time. It will ensure Active Directory and management traffic to our Management OS.

2. The second NIC will ensure Live Migration of virtual machines between our cluster nodes.

3. The third NIC will be used for VM traffic. Our virtual machines will be connected to the various production and lab networks through this NIC.

4. The fourth NIC will be used for internal cluster communication. The first four NICs can either be teamed through Windows Server NIC Teaming or can be abstracted from the physical hardware through to Windows Server network virtualization and converged fabric design.

5. The fifth NIC will be reserved for storage communication. As advised, we will be isolating storage and production LAN communication from each other. If you do not use iSCSI or SMB3 storage communication, this NIC will not be necessary. If you use Fibre Channel SAN technology, use a FC-HBA instead. If you leverage **Direct Attached Storage** (**DAS**), use the appropriate connector for storage communication.

6. The sixth NIC will also be used for storage communication as a redundancy. The redundancy will be established via MPIO and not via NIC Teaming.

There is no need for a dedicated heartbeat network as in older revisions of Windows Server with Hyper-V. All cluster networks will automatically be used for sending heartbeat signals throughout the other cluster members.

If you don't have 1 Gb/s interfaces available, or if you use 10 GbE adapters, it's best practice to implement a converged networking solution described in *Chapter 5, Network Best Practices*.

Storage design

All cluster nodes must have access to the virtual machines residing on a centrally shared storage medium. This could be a classic setup with a SAN, a NAS, or a more modern concept with Windows Scale Out File Servers hosting Virtual Machine Files SMB3 Fileshares. Study *Chapter 4, Storage Best Practices*, for more information on finding the right storage solution for you. In this chapter, we will use a NetApp SAN system that's capable of providing a classic SAN approach with LUNs mapped to our Hosts as well as utilizing SMB3 Fileshares, but any other Windows Server 2012 R2 validated SAN will fulfill the requirements.

In our first setup, we will utilize **Cluster Shared Volumes (CSVs)** to store several virtual machines on the same storage volume. It's not good these days to create a single volume per virtual machine due to a massive management overhead. It's a good rule of thumb to create one CSV per cluster node; in larger environments with more than eight hosts, a CSV per two to four cluster nodes. To utilize CSVs, follow these steps:

1. Ensure that all components (SAN, Firmware, HBAs, and so on) are validated for Windows Server 2012 R2 and are up to date.

2. Connect your SAN physically to all your Hyper-V hosts via iSCSI or Fibre Channel connections.

3. Create two LUNs on your SAN for hosting virtual machines. Activate Hyper-V performance options for these LUNs if possible (that is, on a NetApp, by setting the LUN type to Hyper-V). Size the LUNs for enough capacity to host all your virtual hard disks.

4. Label the LUNs CSV01 and CSV02 with appropriate LUN IDs.

5. Create another small LUN with 1 GB in size and label it Quorum.

6. Make the LUNs available to all Hyper-V hosts in this specified cluster by mapping it on the storage device.

7. Do not make these LUNs available to any other hosts or cluster.

8. Prepare storage DSMs and drivers (that is, MPIO) for Hyper-V host installation.

9. Refresh disk configuration on hosts, install drivers and DSMs, and format volumes as NTFS (quick).

10. Install Microsoft Multipath IO when using redundant storage paths:

```
Install-WindowsFeature -Name Multipath-IO
    -Computername ElanityHV01, ElanityHV02
```

In this example, I added the MPIO feature to two Hyper-V hosts with the computer names `ElanityHV01` and `ElanityHV02`.

SANs typically are equipped with two storage controllers for redundancy reasons. Make sure to disperse your workloads over both controllers for optimal availability and performance.

If you leverage file servers providing SMB3 shares, the preceding steps do not apply to you. Perform the following steps instead:

1. Create a storage space with the desired disk-types, use storage tiering if possible.

2. Create a new SMB3 Fileshare for applications.

3. Customize the Permissions to include all Hyper-V servers from the planned clusters as well as the Hyper-V cluster object itself with full control.

For more details of storage design and configuration, refer to *Chapter 4, Storage Best Practices*.

Server and software requirements

In *Chapter 1, Accelerate Hyper-V Deployment*, you installed your first Hyper-V host. To create a Failover Cluster, you need to install a second Hyper-V host. Use the same unattended file but change the IP address and the hostname. Join both Hyper-V hosts to your Active Directory domain if you have not done this until yet. Hyper-V can be clustered without leveraging Active Directory but it's lacking several key components, such as Live Migration, and shouldn't be done on purpose. The availability to successfully boot up a domain-joined Hyper-V cluster without the need to have any Active Directory domain controller present during boot time is the major benefit from the Active Directory independency of Failover Clusters.

Ensure that you create a Hyper-V virtual switch as shown earlier with the same name on both hosts, to ensure cluster compatibility and that both nodes are installed with all updates.

If you have System Center 2012 R2 in place, use the System Center Virtual Machine Manager to create a Hyper-V cluster (refer to *Chapter 7, Management with System Center*); otherwise, continue with this chapter.

Implementing Failover Clusters

After preparing our Hyper-V hosts, we will now create a Failover Cluster using PowerShell. I'm assuming your hosts are installed, storage and network connections are prepared, and the Hyper-V role is already active utilizing up-to-date drivers and firmware on your hardware.

1. First, we need to ensure that Servername, Date, and Time of our Hosts are correct. Time and Timezone configurations should occur via Group Policy.

2. For automatic network configuration later on, it's important to rename the network connections from default to their designated roles using PowerShell, as seen in the following commands:

   ```
   Rename-NetAdapter -Name "Ethernet" -NewName "Host"

   Rename-NetAdapter -Name "Ethernet 2" -NewName "LiveMig"

   Rename-NetAdapter -Name "Ethernet 3" -NewName "VMs"

   Rename-NetAdapter -Name "Ethernet 4" -NewName "Cluster"

   Rename-NetAdapter -Name "Ethernet 5" -NewName "Storage"
   ```

   The **Network Connections** window should look like the following screenshot:

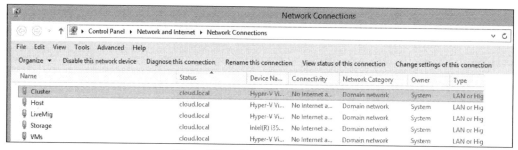

Hyper-V host Network Connections

3. Next, we need to set IP configuration of the network adapters. If you are not using DHCP for your servers, manually set the IP configuration (different subnets) of the specified network cards. Here is a great blog post on how to automate this step: http://bit.ly/Upa5bJ

4. Next, we need to activate the necessary Failover-Clustering features on both of our Hyper-V hosts:

   ```
   Install-WindowsFeature -Name Failover-Clustering
     -IncludeManagementTools -Computername ElanityHV01, ElanityHV02
   ```

5. Before actually creating the cluster, we are launching a cluster validation cmdlet via PowerShell:

```
Test-Cluster ElanityHV01, ElanityHV02
```

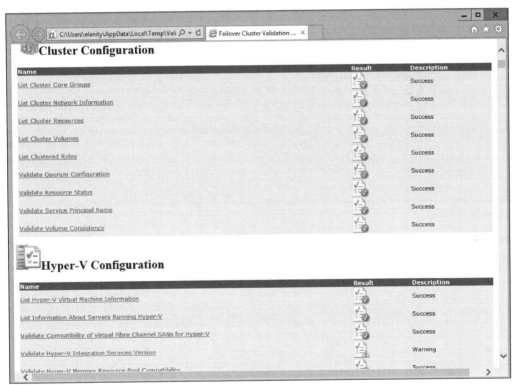

Test-Cluster cmdlet

Open the generated .mht file for more details, as shown in the following screenshot:

Cluster validation

As you can see, there are some warnings that should be investigated. However, as long as there are no errors, the configuration is ready for clustering and fully supported by Microsoft. However, check out `Warnings` to be sure you won't run into problems in the long run. After you have fixed potential errors and warnings listed in the Cluster Validation Report, you can finally create the cluster as follows:

```
New-Cluster
-Name CN=ElanityClu1,OU=Servers,DC=cloud,DC=local
-Node ElanityHV01, ElanityHV02
-StaticAddress 192.168.1.49
```

This will create a new cluster named `ElanityClu1` consisting of the nodes `ElanityHV01` and `ElanityHV02` and using the cluster IP address 192.168.1.49.

This cmdlet will create the cluster and the corresponding Active Directory Object in the specified OU. Moving the cluster object to a different OU later on is no problem at all; even renaming is possible when done the right way.

After creating the cluster, when you open the **Failover Cluster Management** console, you should be able to connect to your cluster:

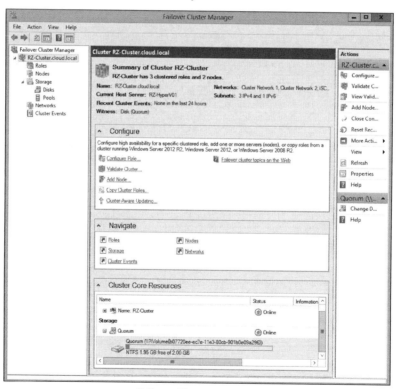

Failover Cluster Manager

You will see that all your **cluster nodes** and `Cluster Core Resources` are online. Rerun the Validation Report and copy the generated `.mht` files to a secure location if you need them for support queries. Keep in mind that you have to rerun this wizard if any hardware or configuration changes occurring to the cluster components, including any of its nodes.

The initial cluster setup is now complete and we can continue with post creation tasks.

Quorum configuration

The quorum is a very important part of a cluster, especially when your cluster has an even number of nodes. The quorum helps to keep the data integrity and avoids split-brain situations. If the network connections between the cluster nodes fail, a cluster node in an even-node setup would have no information if he is part of the isolated area through the outage and has to shut down all cluster services. If it is in the remaining part of the network, it would have to take over cluster services being offline due to the outage. For a successful "vote", which node or nodes are to take over the production service, a total of more than 50 percent of all cluster nodes will need to communicate. If—like in our situation with a two-node cluster—not more than 50 percent of the nodes are available, the node shuts down all its cluster services. In our scenario, both nodes stop all services and our cluster is completely offline to protect us from a split brain situation. A quorum is another instance of getting to "vote" and ensuring majority of cluster resources are available to do a successful vote. In our configuration, the smallest storage volume got assigned as a quorum automatically. That's why we created a 1 GB LUN earlier. Using this LUN as a quorum ensures that there is a majority of votes available in an event that partitions an even-node cluster, such as a network outage.

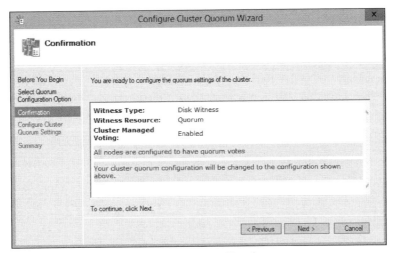

Cluster Quorum Wizard

A quorum can either be a logical disk or a Fileshare. There are several reasons why you should prefer a **Disk Witness** over a Fileshare Witness if possible; for instance, the disk-based witness will host a complete copy of the cluster database Fileshare Witness won't. With the recent version of Hyper-V, you won't have to think about when to choose a quorum and how to configure it. You just specify a Disk Witness if available or a File Share; otherwise, and Failover-Clustering automatically configures the necessary settings — regardless of the number of nodes. If you are currently using a two-node cluster and plan to add more cluster nodes later, you won't have to change the quorum model later. There are options to change the vote counts of the various resources, and it's best practice to not change them in typical cluster configurations. Quorum changes can occur online, we can achieve this through PowerShell:

```
Set-ClusterQuorum -NodeAndDiskMajority "Cluster Disk 2"
```

The preceding line represents `"Cluster Disk 2"` as the label of the Cluster Resource. If you are using a Fileshare, use the following option:

```
Set-ClusterQuorum -NodeAndFileShareMajority \\ElanityFile01\
Share01
```

Live Migration configuration

Live Migration describes the ability to move running virtual machines between Hyper-V hosts. Since Windows Server 2012, this capability is not an exclusive cluster feature anymore, but most of the time they are utilized inside a cluster. You can use Live Migrations between standalone hosts or between different clusters as well: a Shared-Nothing Live Migration will occur, moving not only the RAM of the virtual machine but all of its virtual hard disks, which may consume a lot of network bandwidth and time. Typically, Shared-Nothing Live Migrations are used in migration processes and not in day-to-day work.

A Live Migration of virtual machines occurs every time a planned failover is executed on a Hyper-V cluster. The RAM of the virtual machine is synchronized between the nodes, the handles for the virtual machine configuration and its virtual hard disks are then failed-over to the new host. It's one of the most widely used features in Hyper-V but often seen configured incorrectly.

An important aspect of the Live Migration process is the machine-based authentication. CredSSP is the default authentication protocol in Windows Server 2012 R2 Hyper-V. It is easy to use but it's not the most secure solution and not recommended for production systems. If only one system gets compromised in the chain of delegation, all systems used in the CredSSP environment are compromised as well. Besides that, if you are using CredSSP for Live Migrations, you will have to log on to the source host first to initiate the migration process due to a one hop limitation of CredSSP.

If your Hyper-V hosts are part of the same Active Directory domain—and in most cases they will be—you can use Kerberos protocol for Live Migration authentication, which offers more security and gets around the limitations of CredSSP. Furthermore, it lets you define granular limits where the account credentials can be used. Use PowerShell to set constraint delegations on a system with Active Directory Management tools installed for all Hyper-V hosts involved, with the following script:

```
$Host = "ElanityHV02"

$Domain = "Cloud.local"

Get-ADComputer ElanityHV01 | Set-ADObject -Add @{"msDS-
AllowedToDelegateTo"="Microsoft Virtual System Migration
Service/$Host.$Domain", "cifs/$Host.$Domain","Microsoft Virtual System
Migration Service/$Host", "cifs/$Host"}
```

Make sure to reboot the hosts afterwards so this configuration can become active.

However, this will just allow `ElanityHV01` to delegate its credentials to `ElanityHV02`. You have to do this vice versa on your two-node cluster. For bigger clusters, there is a script that enables all combinations for all your Hyper-V hosts (put them in a single OU, best practice for many reasons) at `http://bit.ly/1hC0S9W`.

After we have prepared our Active Directory for Kerberos constraint delegation, we activate incoming and outgoing Live Migrations for our Hyper-V hosts:

```
Enable-VMMigration –Computername ElanityHV01, ElanityHV02

Set-VMHost –Computername ElanityHV01, ElanityHV02
-VirtualMachineMigrationAuthenticationType Kerberos
```

Live Migrations are enabled using compression by default. RAM will be compressed to a ZIP-like archive before transmission and extracted on the target host. This is a great setting if you are using 1 GB/s NICs for Live Migration as it uses spare CPU cycles to compress Live Migrations to speed up the transfer. If you are using 10 GB/s network connections, switch Live Migrations to SMB3 for even better performance. Also, we increase the limit for continuous Live Migrations from two (great for 1 GB/s) to four simultaneous Live Migrations:

```
Set-VMHost -Computername ElanityHV01, ElanityHV02
-MaximumVirtualMachineMigrations 4 -MaximumStorageMigrations 4
-VirtualMachineMigrationPerformanceOption SMBTransport -
```

You can also configure these settings through the GUI of every cluster node:

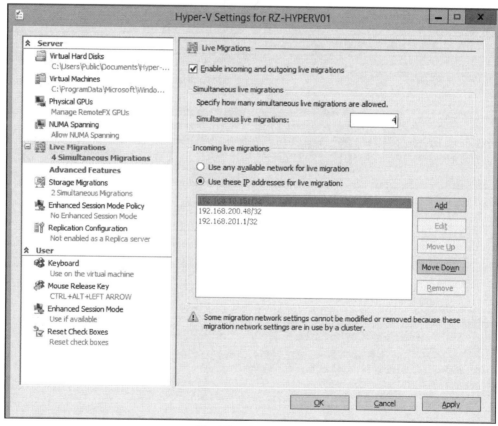

Live Migration options

Use the following command later switch back to the defaults, if needed:

```
Set-VMHost –Computername ElanityHV01, ElanityHV02
-MaximumVirtualMachineMigrations 2 –MaximumStorageMigrations 2
–VirtualMachineMigrationPerformanceOption Compression
```

In the GUI, the preceding command will reflect the changes:

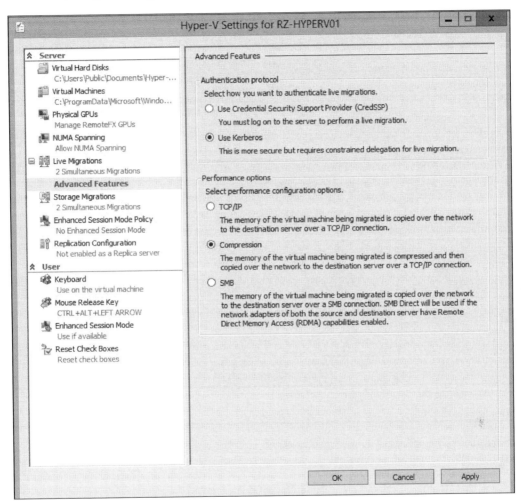

Advanced Live Migration options

The last setting for preparing Live Migrations is to choose the network for Live Migration. By default, all available networks are enabled for Live Migration. We don't change that. If our Live Migration network is unavailable and we quickly need to free up a host, we will use other available networks as well; however, by specifying a lower priority (default is greater than 5.000) to our Live Migration network, we ensure it is preferred for Live Migrations:

```
Set-VMMigrationNework 192.168.10.* -Priority 4.000

(Get-ClusterNetwork -Name "Live-Migration").Role = 1
```

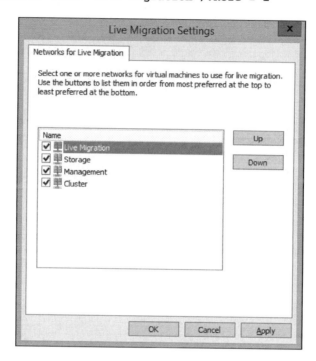

We also set the basic configuration for the other cluster networks:

```
(Get-ClusterNetwork -Name "Management ").Role = 3

Set-VMMigrationNework 192.168.10.* -Priority 4.000

(Get-ClusterNetwork -Name "Cluster").Role = 1

(Get-ClusterNetwork -Name "Cluster").Metric = 3.000

(Get-ClusterNetwork -Name "Storage").Role = 0
```

The final network configuration should now look like the following screenshot:

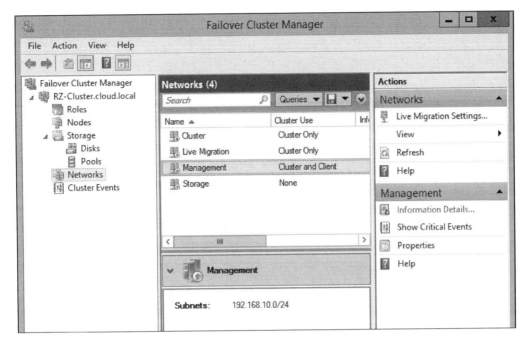

After that configuration, we are ready to initiate our first Live Migration. To do this, simply execute on our first host:

```
Move-VM "VM01" ElanityHV02
```

If you want to Live Migrate all virtual machines from one host to another, use the following cmdlet:

```
Suspend-ClusterNode -Name ElanityHV01 -Target ElanityHV02 –Drain
```

We are now finished with the configuration of our host-cluster. For more advanced monitoring and tuning configurations for Failover Clusters, refer to *Chapter 6, Hyper-V Performance Tuning*.

You are now ready to test your cluster configuration before putting it into production. Power off a running cluster node hosting virtual machines by removing the power cables and see what's happening to your cluster. Do not use the Shutdown command or the buttons on the server as this would not be a real-life test.

Guest clustering

After creating a Hyper-V Failover Cluster on the host level, it is now time to create a guest cluster. A guest cluster is also a Failover Cluster and works the same way as our host-cluster; however, it's hosting applications are on top of operating systems instead of virtual machine workloads. A guest cluster is used in conjunction to a host-cluster to ensure an even higher availability. Do not create guest clusters unless you are already using a host-cluster, it won't increase availability to your services in a hardware failure scenario; however, they are great for planned failovers for maintenance purposes on one node.

The basic concepts and the cluster creation are identical to the host-cluster, that is, running the Cluster Validation Wizard successfully in order to receive support. However, with two running VMs hosting the same service, that is, a production ERP application, you should avoid that these two VMs are running on the same physical node on your Hyper-V cluster. You can achieve this using anti-affinity rules that makes sure of placing the VMs on different hosts. This is possible via System Center Virtual Machine Manager (refer to *Chapter 7, Management with System Center*) or with PowerShell. It is not possible with Failover Cluster Manager GUI. We will continue with the PowerShell approach for now. To create a new anti-affinity rule, execute the following command:

```
(Get-ClusterGroup ERP-VM1).AntiAffinityClassNames = "GuestClusterERP1"
(Get-ClusterGroup ERP-VM2).AntiAffinityClassNames = "GuestClusterERP1"
```

These VMs won't be placed on the same host if possible. Check your current anti-affinity rules affecting a virtual machine by executing the following command:

```
Get-ClusterGroup VM1 | fl anti*
```

Network design for a guest cluster

Since we are already running in a virtual world, our network setup for our guest cluster is simplified. We just need three types of networks instead of five:

- **Client network**: This is used for Client Connections to our applications and should be configured with Role = 0
- **Cluster network**: This network serves the same purpose as on the host-cluster; configure it with the equivalent values
- **Storage network**: This network serves the same purpose as on the host-cluster; configure it with the equivalent values

These networks need to be configured on the guest cluster additionally to any host-cluster networks.

It's best practice in a guest-cluster environment to change the default failover-triggering heartbeat times to allow executing Live Migrations without any cluster activities. To change this from 10 seconds (default value and suitable for physical clusters) to 25 seconds (TCP time out of Live Migrations are typically up to 20 seconds), execute the following PowerShell cmdlet:

```
(Get-Cluster).CrossSubnetThreshold = 25
(Get-Cluster).SameSubnetThreshold = 25
```

Storage design for a guest cluster

While our network setup benefits from the virtual world, the storage design is more complicated through an added layer of complexity. Just like our host-cluster, the guest cluster needs shared storage between the two virtual machines, leaving us with the following storage options:

- **Shared VHDX**: This new feature of Windows Server 2012 R2 allows multiple VMs to connect to a single virtual hard disk if it's prepared accordingly

- **Virtual Fibre Channel**: This new feature of Windows Server 2012 allows us to pass through a Fibre Channel SAN LUN to virtual machines if you are using FC storage

- **iSCSI**: Connect to a iSCSI target with the iSCSI Initiator from within the VM if you are using iSCSI storage

The last two storage options are explained further in *Chapter 4, Storage Best Practices*. We will use a shared VHDX file to create our Failover Cluster:

1. Create two virtual machines with the Failover-Clustering feature enabled and place them on your cluster shared volumes.

2. Create two new shared VHDX through PowerShell — one for data and one for cluster quorum purposes:

```
New-VHD -Path C:\ClusterStorage\Volume1\VMERPHA_Shared.VHDX -Fixed
-SizeBytes 60GB Add-VMHardDiskDrive -VMName VMERP01 -Path C:\
ClusterStorage\Volume1\VMERPHA_Shared.VHDX
 -ShareVirtualDisk

Add-VMHardDiskDrive -VMName VMERP02 -Path C:\ClusterStorage\
Volume1\VMERPHA_Shared.VHDX
 -ShareVirtualDisk

New-VHD -Path C:\ClusterStorage\Volume1\VMERPHA_quorum.VHDX
 -Fixed -SizeBytes 1GB

Add-VMHardDiskDrive -VMName VMERP01 -Path C:\ClusterStorage\
Volume1\VMERPHA_quorum.VHDX
 -ShareVirtualDisk
```

```
Add-VMHardDiskDrive -VMName VMERP02 -Path C:\ClusterStorage\
Volume1\VMERPHA_quorum.VHDX
 -ShareVirtualDisk
```

3. Create the guest cluster using the shared VHDX file as central storage. Install your application to host all data on the shared storage.

You should choose a shared VHDX when using SMB3 storage since you are not connecting any LUNs to your Hyper-V clusters directly. Since shared VHDX files come with some limitations, such as not supporting host-based Hyper-V backups or storage migrations, these should not be your primary option outside SMB3 configurations.

Cluster-Aware Updating

Since you are able to move running workloads between our cluster nodes without affecting production application performance, we will now add **Cluster-Aware Updating (CAU)**, allowing our Hyper-V cluster to install updates by itself. This is a must-have configuration to ensure low maintenance operations of your Hyper-V clusters. CAU will automatically download and install updates to all cluster nodes utilizing Live Migrations. This way we can update our cluster at any time of the day without the need for service downtime Execute the following cmdlet on one of the cluster nodes:

```
Add-CauClusterRole -ClusterName CAUElanityHA-01 -Force -CauPluginName
Microsoft.WindowsUpdatePlugin -MaxRetriesPerNode 3 -CauPluginArguments @
{ 'IncludeRecommendedUpdates' = 'True' } -StartDate "5/6/2014 3:00:00 AM"
-DaysOfWeek 4 -WeeksOfMonth @(3) -verbose
```

You can even utilize an existing WSUS-Server as updating clusters never has been easier. There is additional guidance available around CAU in the Altaro blog at http://bit.ly/Vl7y24.

Summary

With the knowledge from this chapter, you are now able to design and implement Hyper-V Failover Clusters as well as guest clusters. You are aware of the basic concepts of High Availability and the storage and networking options necessary to achieve this. You have seen real-world proven configurations to ensure a stable operating environment.

Continue now to *Chapter 3, Backup and Disaster Recovery*, to ensure your services are still running if a disaster occurs and be prepared to recover your data!

3
Backup and Disaster Recovery

Whether you are using Windows Server Backup, Azure Backup, Azure Site Recovery, Hyper-V Replica, or any third-party data protection solution, you need to clearly define your RTO and RPO goals and adapt your strategy with a new technology that understands your virtualization platform. The days of a single solution fits all are also over, only a layered approach with different technologies will give you the benefits and SLAs you need, and top of that, they can assist you in your day-to-day work also.

Mike Resseler – MVP Hyper-V

Being prepared when a data loss occurs, caused by human error or a technical disaster, is important. Your business needs to continue running after such an impact. Running all or even the most important virtual machines is typically a needful resource for your business. This chapter will make you familiar with backup methods of Hyper-V hosts and VMs and continues with Hyper-V Replica as Hyper-V's primary disaster recovery component. You will also learn how to automate a complete end-to-end disaster recovery process.

This chapter includes the following topics:

- Hyper-V Replica and extension
- Azure Site Recovery Manager
- Windows Server Backup and Hyper-V

Protecting a Hyper-V environment

Preparing for a situation that hopefully never takes place. This is the kind of definition for backup and disaster recovery. While a restore of a lost word document on a file server is a common and well-practiced task occurring daily in most IT environments, the complete loss of a bunch of VMs or even a whole Hyper-V cluster is unlikely to occur—you think. Almost all companies make use of redundant components, and even clusters are standard; however, **Single Points of Failures (SPOFs)** can often be found. The following are a few examples:

- Non-mirrored storage systems
- Core switches
- Intersite networking
- Authentication systems

So, a typical technical architecture offers a realistic chance for a disaster to occur. Hardware and software issues aren't the number one on the list of possible disaster scenarios. More than 50 percent of all disastrous issues are triggered by a human error according to backup-focused company Acronis. Deleting the wrong VM, provisioning wipe commands against production environments instead of lab systems, mistyped IP addresses, or simply the classic staff stumbling over the wrong set of cables happens very fast and very often. In the previous chapter, you learned a lot about High Availability. You cannot prepare your Hyper-V environment to withstand any kind of problem without a service interruption. You have to decide for which disasters to prepare and which risks you want to take. Let's jump to the point where all your High Availability efforts have failed: it's disaster time.

Hyper-V Replica

The core feature of Hyper-V disaster recovery technologies is Hyper-V Replica: the ability to replicate a virtual machine near real time to another Hyper-V host. On the second host, an offline copy of the virtual machine is created and updated every 30 seconds or alternatively, every few minutes with changed blocks from the running source-VM. Both physical machines host nearly identical copies of the same virtual machine with the same name, the same IP address, and the same content. Optional VSS consistency provides additional data integrity throughout the replication process. The replicated VM is offline until a disaster takes place and the VM will be powered up (manually) when it's needed. Both hosts don't have to use identical hardware, storage systems, or Active Directory domains. Instead of restoring up to 24-hour-old data from your backup, the maximum data loss in this scenario is only a few minutes of data.

In the case of a broken SAN, you will decrease the mean time to return to production from your old timeframe:

1. Identify the problem—30 minutes.
2. SAN Replacement SLA—8 hours.
3. Restore terabytes of data from the Tier 2 backup archive—48 hours.

Just power on the virtual machines on the replica host and after their boot is completed, you are back in production. The replication between the virtual machines is automatically reversed. All changes to your virtual machine in a disaster situation are replicated back to the source VM when it becomes available again. After restoring the primary hardware, wait for the replication to complete and switch back in a controlled process to the primary systems. This process will need a short downtime but will occur without data loss.

You can replicate between standalone hosts, between clusters, and even between standalone hosts and a cluster. You cannot replicate between hosts that are members of the same cluster because the replica virtual machine is an exact copy of the original, and you cannot have duplicates within the cluster. Hyper-V Replica is an ideal candidate to be considered for data redundancy and disaster compute resources. If possible, place the Replica-hosts on another site or even another geographic region. It's possible to replicate over WAN to another data center or Microsoft's public cloud. There are several automation options available for Hyper-V Replica, that is, PowerShell and Azure Site Recovery Manager (both covered in this chapter), as well as System Center 2012 R2 with its Orchestrator Component (covered in *Chapter 7, Management with System Center*).

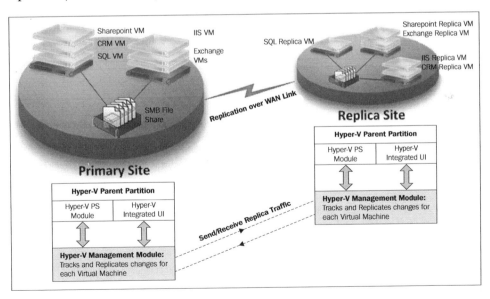

It's best practice to use slower/older hardware and a cheaper storage architecture on Replica sites when they are only used as Replica-targets. If you have non-production systems such as development or lab-VMs, move them to your Replica-targets and shut them down in a disaster scenario. If you have identical hardware setups on both sides, host VMs on both sites and configure a crossover replication between the hosts.

Enabling Hyper-V Replica

To enable Hyper-V Replica for your existing virtual machines, we follow a five-step process as follows:

1. Prepare the first host for sending replication data and receiving data in a disaster scenario.

2. Enable the Replica-hosts to receive replication data and send data in a disaster scenario.

3. Activate replication on selected virtual machines and configure the replication scenario.

4. Monitor the replication.

5. Test Hyper-V Replica.

Preparing the first host

Our Hyper-V installation does not allow the replication of virtual machines by default and Hyper-V Replica needs to be enabled:

Start an elevated PowerShell and execute the following command:

```
Set-VMReplicationServer -AllowedAuthenticationType kerberos
-ReplicationEnabled 1
```

To enable this on multiple hosts, use and also set the default location for incoming replications:

```
Set-VMReplicationServer -AllowedAuthenticationType kerberos
-ReplicationEnabled 1-ComputerName "ElanityHost01", "ElanityHost02"
-DefaultStorageLocation "C:\ClusterStorage\Volume1\Hyper-V Replica"
```

The default authentication method used with Hyper-V Replica is Kerberos. Use Kerberos in an already secured environment if all participating hosts are joined to the same Active Directory domain. If you are replicating over WAN connections or have different domains (Replica is truly independent of Active Directory domains), switch to certificate-based authentication, which also adds encrypted data transfers:

```
Set-VMReplicationServer -ReplicationEnabled 1 -AllowedAuthenticationType
Certificate
 -CertificateAuthenticationPort 8000 -CertificateThumbprint
"0442C676C8726ADDD1CE029AFC20EB158490AFC8"
```

Replace the certificate thumbprint with the corresponding one from the certificate you want to use. The equivalent certificate with it's private key must be present on all involved hosts. Use an existing trusted certificate authority to create the certificates and GPOs to distribute them to the corresponding hosts. Use a certificate template for server authentication when issuing certificates to your Hyper-V hosts. Use the server's FQDN as the subject name. However, if no existing CA is available or can be set up, I recommend using Makecert to create a self-signed certificate quickly and easily. Obtain the tool and the instructions to create self signed certificates for Hyper-V Replica at `http://bit.ly/YmgzK3`.

If you are using Hyper-V hosts in a Failover Cluster, the replica configuration is only needed once per cluster. To achieve this, create a Hyper-V Replica Broker role via elevated PowerShell:

```
Add-ClusterServerRole -Name Replica-Broker -StaticAddress 192.168.1.5
```

```
Add-ClusterResource -Name "Virtual Machine Replication Broker" -Type
"Virtual Machine Replication Broker" -Group Replica-Broker
```

```
Add-ClusterResourceDependency "Virtual Machine Replication Broker"
Replica-Broker
```

```
Start-ClusterGroup Replica-Broker
```

Keep in mind that when using certificate-based authentication, you need to issue additional certificates with the FQDN of the Hyper-V Broker role to all Hyper-V hosts. To enable successful replications to our hosts later on, we need to prepare the running Windows Firewall. Do this via GPO or run the following PowerShell script once in a cluster for Kerberos-based authentication:

```
get-clusternode | ForEach-Object  {Invoke-command -computername $_.name
-scriptblock {Enable-Netfirewallrule -displayname "Hyper-V Replica HTTP
Listener (TCP-In)"}}
```

Also, run the following script for certificate-based authentication:

```
get-clusternode | ForEach-Object  {Invoke-command -computername $_.name
-scriptblock {Enable-Netfirewallrule -displayname "Hyper-V Replica HTTPS
Listener (TCP-In)"}}
```

By default, Hyper-V Replica allows incoming replications from all servers. It's best practice to filter this to only the corresponding replication hosts. First, enable selective replication as follows:

```
Set-VMReplicationServer -AllowedAuthenticationType kerberos
-ReplicationEnabled 1 -ComputerName "ElanityHost01", "ElanityHost02"
-DefaultStorageLocation "C:\ClusterStorage\Volume1\Hyper-V Replica"-
ReplicationAllowedFromAnyServer 0
```

Then, use the following:

```
New-VMReplicationAuthorizationEntry -AllowedPrimaryServer ElanityHost01.
elanity.local -ReplicaStorageLocation C:\ClusterStorage\Volume1\ -
TrustGroup EYGroup01 -ComputerName ElanityHost02.elanity.local
```

Where `TrustGroup` is a logical group. Add all corresponding replication hosts and brokers to the same security tag. You can use wildcard characters for a particular domain without having to specify all hosts individually (for example, `*.elanity.com`).

After that, our first Hyper-V host or cluster is ready to use Hyper-V Replica.

Preparing additional hosts

Repeat the steps for additional hosts, if you are using a more standalone Hyper-V server. Make sure to use consistent trust groups/security tags.

The GUI should reflect your changes as shown in the following screenshot:

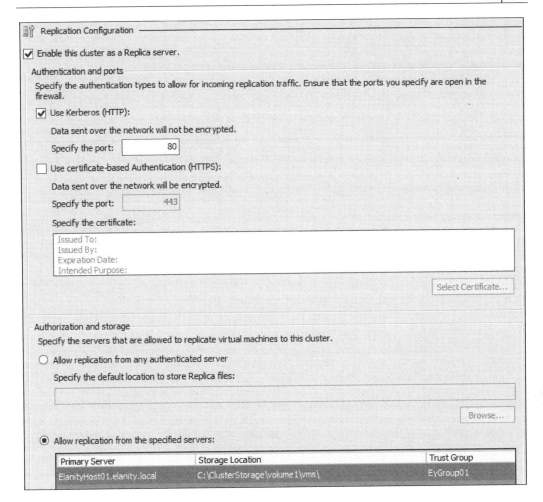

```
Replication Configuration

☑ Enable this cluster as a Replica server.

  Authentication and ports
    Specify the authentication types to allow for incoming replication traffic. Ensure that the ports you specify are open in the
    firewall.
    ☑ Use Kerberos (HTTP):
       Data sent over the network will not be encrypted.
       Specify the port:        80
    ☐ Use certificate-based Authentication (HTTPS):
       Data sent over the network will be encrypted.
       Specify the port:        443
       Specify the certificate:
       ┌──────────────────────────────────────────────────────────┐
       │ Issued To:                                                 │
       │ Issued By:                                                 │
       │ Expiration Date:                                           │
       │ Intended Purpose:                                          │
       └──────────────────────────────────────────────────────────┘
                                                    [ Select Certificate... ]

  Authorization and storage
  Specify the servers that are allowed to replicate virtual machines to this cluster.

  ○ Allow replication from any authenticated server
    Specify the default location to store Replica files:
    ┌──────────────────────────────────────────────────────────┐
    │                                                            │
    └──────────────────────────────────────────────────────────┘
                                                        [ Browse... ]

  ◉ Allow replication from the specified servers:
```

Primary Server	Storage Location	Trust Group
ElanityHost01.elanity.local	C:\ClusterStorage\volume1\vms\	EyGroup01

Activate VM replication

The replication of VMs is configured on a per VM basis; typically, you select all production VMs for replication. Keep using PowerShell to configure this efficiently.

Run the following PowerShell cmdlets from an elevated Shell to replicate the EYVM01 virtual machine to host EyHost02:

```
Set-VMReplication –VMName EYVM01 –ReplicaServerName EyHost02.elanity.
local –ReplicaServerPort 80
```

This is all the configuration needed to prepare the replication. Start the initial replication by executing the following command:

```
Start-VMInitialReplication -VMName EYVM01
```

The replication is started and all set to go. However, there is a great set of recommended options to customize the replica configuration.

By adding `-CompressionEnabled 1`, all replication traffic gets compressed before its replication occurs. The very small amount of CPU cycles needed to compress and extract the packets is a great trade-off to a lot of expensive bandwidth saving and is highly recommended.

```
Start-VMInitialReplication -VMName EYVM01 -CompressionEnabled 1
```

The initial replication can be a huge amount of data. To not overwhelm the network or WAN bandwidth, it can be scheduled to occur at a specific time by adding the following:

```
-InitialReplicationStartTime 5/1/2014 7:00 AM
```

A great parameter I recommend to add is as follows:

```
-RecoveryHistory 24 to the Set-VMReplication CMDlet
```

This ensures that not only the current replica of the virtual machine is stored on the replica server but the last 24 Versions of the virtual machine. This is incredibly useful if the primary VMs are hit by a logical error such as a computer virus. The virus will be replicated near real time into your disaster-ready VMs. Just power off the source VMs and reboot an older recovery point, that is, 2 hours back in time, where you are sure the virus is not yet present. In this way, you can recover from a destructive computer virus or human error in minutes instead of days.

Set the replication frequency to 30, 300, or 900 seconds. I recommend to use 30 seconds as a default value for the first 50 VMs. When replicating more than 50 VMs, switch to 300 seconds as your default, due to increased system resources used for replication. If one replication window is missed or the replica window needs longer than your replication interval, it will continue with the next available replication window:

```
-ReplicationFrequencySec 30
```

To ensure application consistency, add regular VSS snapshots to our replication by adding the following:

```
-VSSSnapshotFrequencyHour 4
```

Which will ensure occurring VSS snapshots every 4 hours.

The final PowerShell Script should look like the following script:

```
Set-VMReplication -VMName EYVM01 -ReplicaServerName EyHost02.elanity.
local -ReplicaServerPort 80 -RecoveryHistory 24 -ReplicationFrequencySec
30 -VSSSnapshotFrequencyHour 4

Start-VMInitialReplication -VMName EYVM01 -CompressionEnabled 1
-InitialReplicationStartTime 5/1/2014 7:00 AM
```

Activate this for the virtual machines you want to protect for disaster recovery.

It is best practice to move temporary files to a different virtual hard disk and exclude it from replication to save bandwidth and ensure fast replication times. The Windows Pagefile is a great example for a temp file not needed on the replica site. There is a great TechNet blogpost on this topic. For details, visit http://bit. ly/1pDtq4P.

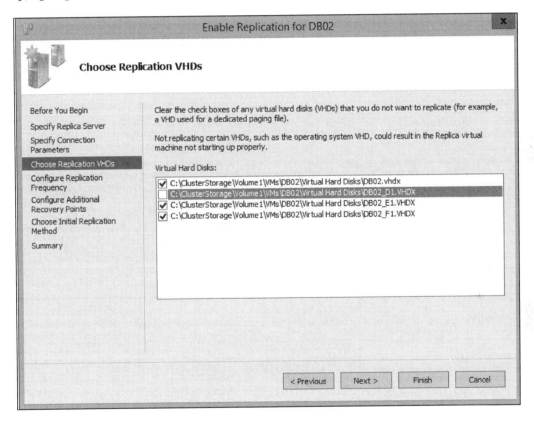

Hyper-V Replica is fully compatible with Windows Server Network Virtualization and its Quality of Service settings. It's a great way to throttle Replica-traffic during office peak hours. Refer to *Chapter 5, Network Best Practices*, for details.

The configuration shown to implement Hyper-V Replica can also be done in the GUI of Windows Server. However, for scaling purposes, you should prefer PowerShell. To automate the whole process, use the following script to configure Hyper-V Replica between two hosts:

```
$HVSource = "EyHost01"

$HVReplica = "EyHost02"

$Port = 80

$HVdisabld = get-vm -ComputerName $HVSource | where {$_.replicationstate -eq 'disabled' }

foreach ($VM in $HVdisabld) {

  enable-VMReplication $VM $Replica $Port $Auth

Set-VMReplication -VMName $VM.name  -ReplicaServerName $HVReplica -ReplicaServerPort $Port -AuthenticationType kerberos -CompressionEnabled $true -RecoveryHistory 0 -computername $HVSource

Start-VMInitialReplication $VM.name  -ComputerName $HVSource
```

Monitoring Hyper-V Replica

Use `Measure-VMReplication | format-list *` to get details of the current replication processes. Use System Center Operations Manager for a complete health-monitoring of Hyper-V Replica:

```
Name                              : contoso2
Id                                : 61388695-555a-49d2-9f14-26886eca9edb
State                             : Replicating
Health                            : Normal
LReplTime                         : 18-3-2012 15:24:24
PReplSize                         : 4096
AvgLatency                        : 00:01:07
AvgReplSize                       : 5369016576
SuccReplCount                     : 2
CurrentTask                       : {}
MonitoringStartTime               : 18-3-2012 15:06:28
MonitoringEndTime                 : 18-3-2012 15:25:42
LastReplicationType               : None
FailedOverReplicationType         : None
LastTestFailoverInitiatedTime     :
LastVSSSnapshotTime               :
InitialReplicationSize            : 0
PendingReplicationSize            : 4096
AverageReplicationSize            : 5369016576
MaximumReplicationSize            : 10736369664
AverageReplicationLatency         : 00:01:07
MaximumReplicationLatency         : 00:02:15
ReplicationErrors                 : 0
SuccessfulReplicationCount        : 2
MissedReplicationCount            : 0
ComputerName                      : VMHOST2
PrimaryServerName                 : VMHOST2.contoso.com
CurrentReplicaServerName          : vmhost1.contoso.com
ReplicaServerName                 : vmhost1.contoso.com
ReplicationState                  : Replicating
ReplicationHealth                 : Normal
ReplicationMode                   : Primary
LastReplicationTime               : 18-3-2012 15:24:24
ReplicatedDisks                   : {Hard Drive on IDE controller number 0 at location 0}
SecurityTag                       :
TestVirtualMachine                :
VMId                              : 61388695-555a-49d2-9f14-26886eca9edb
VMName                            : contoso2
IsDeleted                         : False
```

Hyper-V Replica testing and failover

There are multiple options to test whether your replica is working. Execute a planned failover for switching one VM without data loss to the replica node. Be aware, this involves a short downtime of the VM.

```
Stop-VM -VMName EyVM1 -ComputerName ElanityHost01

Start-VMFailover -VMName EYVM01 -ComputerName ElanityHost01-Prepare
```

The preceding command stops the original VMs and prepares both hosts for a planned failover. Execute the following:

```
Start-VMFailover -VMName EYVM01 -ComputerName ElanityHost02  -as Test

for forcing a planned failover.
```

If your disaster takes place, just remove the `-as Test` to start the real failover, and reverse the replication with:

```
Set-VMReplication -VMName  EyVM01 -ComputerName ElanityHost02  -Reverse
```

The question I get asked most often is how to automate this failover process. I strongly recommend to do only manual failovers to avoid split brain situations where the same VM is powered on accidently on both sites. However, for scripting, this in an on-premise situation. For more details, visit `http://bit.ly/1sn0m4y` or use the Azure Site Recovery service that is covered later in this chapter.

Another great way to test your replica is to do a test failover. This creates a copy of selected virtual machines in an isolated environment without affecting the production service. This way, you can test the replicated VM without any time constraints. Visit `http://bit.ly/1niNnK6` for more information on different failover types.

In a testing scenario or at a disaster site, it may be necessary to alter the IP configuration of the replicated virtual machines due to other subnets being used at that site:

```
Set-VMNetworkAdapterFailoverConfiguration EYVM01'

-IPv4Address 192.168.1.1

-IPv4SubnetMask 255.255.255.0

-IPv4DefaultGateway 192.168.1.254
```

To change the vSwitch of the VM for a test failover, use the following:

```
Set-VMNetworkAdapter ,EYVM01'

-TestReplicaSwitchName 'vSwitchTest01'
```

Have a look at the GUI representation of these options in the following screenshot:

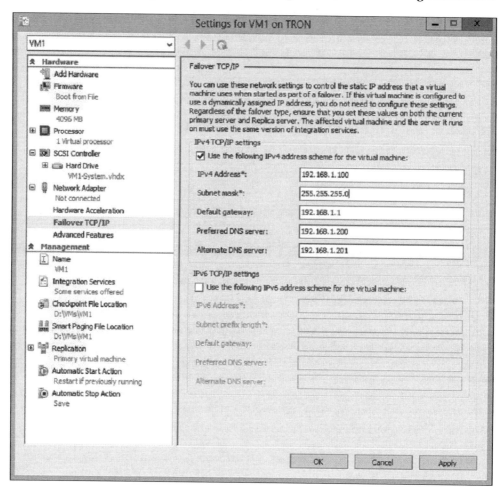

After configuring these options, you are all set for widespread disaster recovery with Hyper-V Replica. You can even configure your replica VM to extend another replication to a third site, for instance, a Partner Datacenter.

Azure Site Recovery

With Azure Site Recovery, Microsoft offers a complete end-to-end solution (formerly known as Hyper-V Recovery Manager). Install two Hyper-V hosts as you have learned in the previous chapters, do not cluster them, but add them to one or two instances of System Center Virtual Machine Manager 2012/2012 R2.

Log on to a Microsoft Azure subscription, use a trial subscription if you have none, and create a new Azure Site Recovery Vault that will host all replica-related information. Visit `http://bit.ly/1v61J50` for details.

1. Upload a certificate to the created Site Recovery Vault. Again, use an existing CA if available or create a computer authentication certificate via Makecert. Make sure to upload only the public key of the certificate. Visit `http://bit.ly/1kMP1X3` for details.

2. Install the Azure Site Recovery Provider on your SCVMM Server. Visit `http://bit.ly/1pVcEgc` for details.

3. Install the Azure Recovery Services Agent on each Hyper-V host. Visit `http://bit.ly/1rKDIOQ` for details.

4. You can now control these hosts through Microsoft's public cloud, Microsoft Azure. With Azure Site Recovery, you can enable Hyper-V Replica, configure its authentication and replication options, and select groups of VMs (SCVMM Clouds). All the selected virtual machines will be enabled for Hyper-V Replica automatically and you can even set options for automatic failover processes. In this case, only the orchestration and management is done through Microsoft Azure. You can now even select Microsoft Azure as a storage target for Hyper-V Replica. Incoming network traffic to Azure is free, so this is very a cost-effective solution compared to building another data center to host backup systems. Visit `http://bit.ly/1kMQiyt` for details.

5. Map your on-premise networks used by virtual machines to the corresponding Azure networks. Visit `http://bit.ly/1pvlJND` for details.

6. Build and test recovery plans. Build logical groups of VMs to define the order in which VMs are starting, including a slight delay between the groups so that you can start your Active Directory before your database servers and start your ERP Server after all databases are online. A virtual machine is only built from the replicated storage data when there is an emergency and a failover to Azure occurs. Welcome to a real hybrid cloud scenario. Visit `http://bit.ly/1yOTlap` for details.

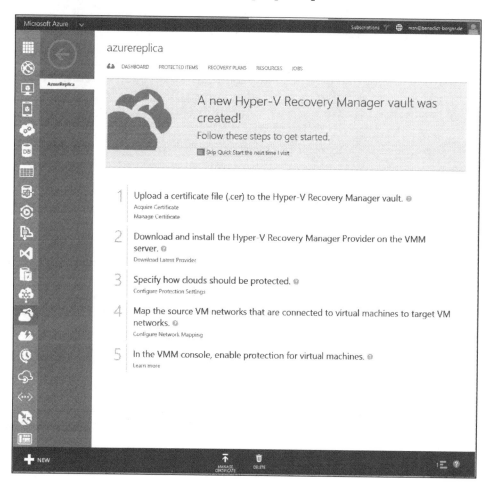

Replica workloads

Before you now start to mirror all your virtual machines at a cost, please keep in mind that your workload needs to be able to handle the failover mechanisms of Hyper-V Replica. Hyper-V Replica requires all applications running inside replicated VMs to be able to handle an unplanned power-off of the VM, because this is exactly what happens in an unplanned failover scenario. Most applications have no problem with this, including current versions of Windows Server Domain Controllers hosting Active Directory and Microsoft SQL Servers. Other applications such as Microsoft's Lync or Exchange Server are currently not supported in conjunction with Hyper-V Replica. Both applications however do provide great application-specific HA and DR mechanics that should be leveraged instead.

Backup of virtual machines

A disaster recovery solution such as Hyper-V Replica protects you from a lot of catastrophic scenarios; however, it's not a substitution for a successful backup. Hyper-V backup solutions shifted away from the classic grandfather-father-son backup schedule with nightly backups of every system. Modern Hyper-V backup solutions such as Microsoft's Data Protection Manager work host-based on a block level and track every change happening to any VM that it's included in a backup. These changes are saved as an incremental, continual backup running every 15 minutes. These ensure a quick backup, a fast restore, and reduce data loss in the case of a recovery to a maximum of 15 minutes. Most **Recovery Point Objectives (RPO)** and **Recovery Time Objectives (RTO)** backup SLAs can be met easily with a powerful backup tool. Be careful and choose only a backup tool that is specifically tested with Windows Server 2012 R2 Hyper-V and Cluster Shared Volumes/SMB3 shares. Today, there are many backup solutions on the market that are not capable of this, including the former market leader of infrastructure backup.

After you have implemented your backup tool successfully, make sure to test the recovery of virtual machines on a regular basis. It is very important for that to work so that you keep your backup software on a latest patch level like every other component in your Hyper-V environment.

For a successful backup, its very important that your VSS providers are working and that the integration services of every VM are up to date. To ensure successful backup solutions, make sure you have as few Hyper-V checkpoints enabled on your VMs as possible. A huge chain of checkpoints does endanger the integrity of the running VM and its backups. Also, it's still the best practice to keep a set of backups offsite in case of a real disaster. Here, an interesting option comes into play: because a Hyper-V Replica-protected VM produces an exact copy of the VM, but powered off, which is a great source for backups. Without affecting the production environment and without any VSS-related problems, taking backups from the Replica-VM simplifies offsite backups as well as branch office scenarios. Simply replicate VMs from your branch office to your central data center and include the Replica-VMs in your primary backup.

For smaller environments, even the Windows Server Backup (`wbadmin.exe`) is capable of running host-based Hyper-V backups. Windows Server Backup needs to be enabled first before it can be used. Run the following PowerShell cmdlet to enable wbadmin from an elevated prompt:

```
Add-WindowsFeature Windows-Server-Backup"
```

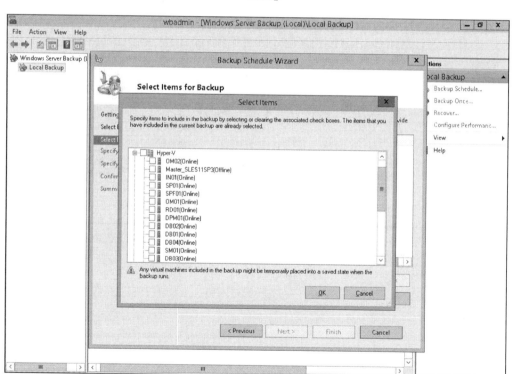

To back up a single virtual machine just use the following command:

```
wbadmin start backup -backupTarget:d:-hyperv:EYVM01 -force
```

To back up the VM `EYVM01` to the local `d:` drive of the host. The VM will stay online during the process as long as current integration services are being used. The `-force` parameter starts the backup immediately without waiting for manual confirmations. wbadmin is capable of storing multiple backups for the same VM when using local storage as a backup target. You can also use network shares as backup target, but old backups will be overwritten.

To restore a backup with wbadmin, you first need to identify the exact date and time of the backup, since it marks the backups version:

```
wbadmin get versions -backupTarget:d:
```

Copy the version identifier shown for your backups and use it in the following command:

```
wbadmin start recover-version:08/18/2014-22:01 -itemType:
hyperv -items:EYVM01-backuptarget:d:
```

To restore the VM `EYVM01` from backup location D:\ with the identified version.

You can back up and restore multiple VMs via wbadmin by a comma separating VM names or virtual machine IDs. Even if you don't have the need to restore your VMs on a regular basis, be sure to test your backups now and then.

A full command-line reference of wbadmin is available at `http://bit.ly/1pHtly0`.

Summary

You now know that High Availability and disaster recovery are two completely different and independent architectures. You can now leverage the best of both worlds and protect your Hyper-V environment from common disasters, even via manual configuration, PowerShell scripting, or through end-to-end solutions such as Azure Site Recovery.

With the knowledge about backup architectures and tools, you are able to secure your virtual machine content even in case of a huge disaster.

Continue now to chapter *Chapter 4, Storage Best Practices*, to learn more about the great new storage options that are around with Windows Server 2012 R2 and Hyper-V.

4

Storage Best Practices

The Windows High Available Fileserver (commonly called Scale-Out Fileserver), Storage Spaces, and of course SMB3 are three great new technologies that are really promising and work great with Hyper-V. I personally think that the legacy of classic SAN storage systems is over because Software Defined Storage solutions are much more flexible and not nearly as expensive as SAN solutions. So prepare yourself to play/test these new solutions!

Carsten Rachfahl – MVP Hyper-V

This chapter will familiarize you with the common storage architectures that are compatible with Hyper-V and how to use them most efficiently. With Windows Server 2012 R2 and Hyper-V, the Storage Landscape for virtualization changed dramatically. For the earlier versions of Windows Server, an expensive SAN was required for High Performance Cluster Systems. As of today, many alternatives are available for cost efficient, high performance, and High Availability Hyper-V Storage sizing and technologies.

These are the topics we'll be covering in this chapter:

- Hyper-V disk formats and types
- SAN versus **Scale-Out File Server (SOFS)**
- Storage Spaces and tiering
- iSCSI target server
- Deduplication and thin provisioning
- ReFS and Hyper-V

Storage overview

Storage for Hyper-V is not primarily about capacity; it is about performance. Stop thinking in terms of capacities such as Gigabytes and Terabytes of data and calculate in IOPS from now on when Hyper-V Storage options are on the table. Of course, you still need to make sure there is enough capacity available. However, these typically neither influence the design nor the costs on a larger scale since high capacity hard drives are available for a very low price. There are very different approaches for a virtualization storage design.

In older versions of Windows Server and other virtualization products, a NAS system for smaller environments and enterprise-grade SAN systems were used as a storage backend. With a Fibre Channel or iSCSI connection to the Virtualization Server Systems, it provides a central storage for all nodes in a cluster, ensuring capabilities such as VM live migration and Cluster Failover.

The loss of cluster nodes does not impact the integrity and availability of the storage systems. The **Logical Unit Numbers** (**LUNs**) of SAN/NAS systems appear as local drives on the Hyper-V hosts. Traditional architectures came with a one-VM-per-LUN approach, which was dropped in modern approaches for Cluster Shared Volumes that hosts multiple VMs per LUN. SAN systems of NAS systems for small Hyper-V setups are still the most often used storage architecture around these days and are fully supported with the recent version of Hyper-V. The use of Cluster Shared Volumes has been improved a lot and is the default deployment option for storage volumes for Hyper-V on a SAN.

A more modern approach is the use of the onboard capabilities of Windows Server storage management. Leveraging the SMB3 performance and availability options of a Microsoft **Scale-Out File Server** (**SOFS**) with attached JBODs allows you to generate IOPS for Hyper-V on a large scale for a considerably lower price. A Microsoft SOF allows you to utilize the best features you know from a SAN with just one or more physical server systems running Windows Server. You can use traditional storage LUNs behind a SOFS or use Storage Spaces with locally attached hard drives. These hard drives are connected through the system as **just a bunch of disks** (**JBOD**) without the use of a hardware RAID controller.

Availability on the storage level is done on a software level by Windows Server. Storage spaces and JBODs offer scalable performance; they are not just a small business solution. VMs are no longer placed on LUNs; instead, they leverage SMB3 file sharing. Continuously available file sharing allows the use of central File Server clusters with hardware resiliency. If you lose a File Server, the shares hosting Hyper-V VMs will not be interrupted. All VMs keep running, even those that were using the lost File Server just a second ago. A transparent failover kicks in to ensure availability of your Hyper-V storage.

The most cost-effective hardware solution behind a Windows File Server Infrastructure for SMB3 are standard Server systems with SAS-attached JBODs. There is no need for expensive SANs or even a RAID controller to achieve high availability and good performance with SMB3-based file services. Storage Spaces build a full storage virtualization abstraction of the connected disks that are / and is even capable of automatically tiering used SSDs and classic hard drives in the same JBODs for optimal performance.

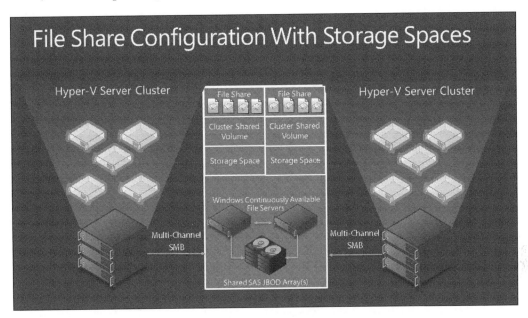

Of course, Hyper-V can also leverage local hard disks in a Server system for the storage of VMs. The VMs can even be replicated to another Hyper-V host in terms of disaster recovery like you learned in *Chapter 3, Backup and Disaster Recovery*, but they do not offer High Availability capabilities and should therefore not be used in production.

SANs versus SOFS

One of the most crucial decisions in a storage design process for Hyper-V is the question of whether to stick with the traditional SAN model or hop on the wagon of Microsoft's SOFS Architecture. Both solutions can do the main job, that is, providing IOPS for VMs, without any problems. Having done many projects using both architectures, the following is some real-world guidance I use for storage design.

The first and most important design principle: do not use nonredundant systems in production for Hyper-V clusters—no local hard drives, no single hardware SMB3-Shares, and no single point of failures on your storage design. If you cannot fulfill these requirements, don't plan for High Availability on Hyper-V. Plan for disaster recovery instead. Uncluster the Hyper-V Servers and replicate the VMs between the nodes in a small setup or between smaller clusters in a bigger environment via Hyper-V Replica. Having said that, let's focus on the decision to make.

Technically, it's possible to use a SOFS in conjunction with a SAN. However, with SAN Vendors adapting SMB3 protocols, this is not an efficient long-term scenario in most cases and we will focus on using SOFS with JBODs and Storage Spaces. There are some SOFS architectures with a SAN you should leverage, particularly, for Fibre Channel SANs, where the Hyper-V hosts may only have Ethernet adapters. Leveraging the SOFS as the entry point to the storage environment reduces the configuration complexity of the "compute" nodes by placing all the storage vendor requirements on the "storage" nodes of the SOFS cluster. You can also place several SANs behind a single SOFS cluster and provide a consistent management and storage presentation experience across the virtualization platform, which will allow you to deploy any variety of storage vendor hardware.

While SAN systems have been around for 15 years, SOFS with Storage Spaces have only been around since Windows Server 2012. If you are working in a large company and have enabled a SAN architecture through your company, including all different applications, operating systems, and requirements, stick with SANs. If you have maintained a uniform storage architecture through all these different areas and have proven processes built around it, do not change this for Hyper-V. Make sure you use Hyper-V-ready SANs with Fibre Channel or iSCSI and continue using them.

In all other design approaches, start under the initial plan of using SOFS. If you find any reason not to use it, switch to a SAN-based solution, but your primary approach should involve SOFS because of its lower price. Don't worry about performance. SOFS/SOF are able to provide more than a million IOPS over 10Gbe-NICs if you really need it (http://www.microsoft.com/en-ie/download/details.aspx?id=42960). SOFS offer Active/Active Cluster configurations leveraging the performance of all storage cluster nodes with the additional benefit of transparent failover. All this is done with Windows Server 2012 capabilities; no third-party additions are necessary. That being said, this is also managed by Windows Server, involving all of the well-known management tools such as Server-Manager and PowerShell. It's way easier to integrate a SOFS in an existing Microsoft environment than a SAN and a lot easier to manage a SOFS than a SAN.

Reasons against a SOFS in a more detailed design process are the advanced requirements. Scale-out File Servers provide you with bare storage for Hyper-V and SQL databases. If you need storage for other purposes, another operating system, or extra capabilities on the storage level such as single item restore without additional backup servers, then a SOFS is not the right solution for you. SOFS, currently, are not able to replicate storage between two or more locations. All SOFS need to be directly attached to the shared JBODs or other storage systems.
To protect against the loss of a JBOD-shelf, keep in mind that you need at least three shelves to avoid split-brain situations. I have seen some production setups with only two shelves filled with hard disks and SSDs, but this setup is not fault-tolerant. Also, SCOFs cannot run in the same cluster like your Hyper-V Cluster does—a separate tier/instance is needed to build SCOFs.

If you want a cheap and fast Windows-based storage solution with SAN-like capabilities, including data deduplication, thin provisioning, and hardware **Offoaded Data Transfer (ODX)**, you are on the right track with Microsoft SOFS. You should prefer SOFS with Storage Spaces. However, if you are currently using a SAN and it does not offer SMB3 capabilities, it may be a good option to use a SOFS in conjunction with the existing SAN.

After choosing one storage architecture, let's now focus on the best practice configurations of Hyper-V technologies.

Storage Spaces and tiering

The best way to leverage a SOFS is to use Storage Spaces with storage tiering. Having JBODs with SSDs and HDDs connected to your SMB3 File Servers enables great I/O performance. Frequently read data will be cached on the SSDs and long-term data will be archived on the HDDs by default without the need for manual editing, which results in a great performance boost. Using the previously explained CSV, a cache can further improve read performance. Create a Storage Space with tiering through PowerShell.

The first step is to create a new storage pool:

```
$PhysicalDisks = Get-PhysicalDisk -CanPool $True

New-StoragePool -FriendlyName ElanityStor01 -StorageSubsystemFriendlyName
"Storage Spaces*" -PhysicalDisks $PhysicalDisks
```

Set the SSD and HDD attributes as follows:

```
$tier_ssd = New-StorageTier -StoragePoolFriendlyName ElanityStor01
-FriendlyName SSD_TIER -MediaType SSD
```

```
$tier_hdd = New-StorageTier -StoragePoolFriendlyName ElanityStor01
-FriendlyName HDD_TIER -MediaType HDD
```

Now you are all set for great storage space performance that you can use with SMB3 shares or combined with SOFS.

If you don't want to put all your trust into the (in my opinion, very nicely working) automatic tiering, you can also manually pin frequently accessed files to the SDD tier:

```
Set-FileStorageTier -FilePath d:\Fastfiles\fast.file -DesiredStorageTier
$tier_ssd
```

Now that we've finished the Storage Space configuration, it's now time to focus on the other aspects of Windows-based storage infrastructure.

Virtual disks

There are several configuration options for virtual hard disks, starting from the disks format. Hyper-V supports, currently, the classic VHD format and the newer VHDX format. VHDX disks are preferable in many ways, starting with their increased size up to 64 Terabyte, over their better performance and reliability options, and to their better management capabilities such as resizing the disks both ways. The only reason to use VHD files now is the backwards compatibility to Hyper-V versions prior to 2012. If you don't need this, don't use VHD files. If you are still using VHD files, convert them via PowerShell when in the offline state:

```
Convert-VHD -Path d:\VM01.vhd -DestinationPath d:\VM01.vhdx
```

After setting the format of the virtual disk, the next decision will be about the type of the virtual disk. Hyper-V supports three types of virtual hard disks:

- Fixed
- Dynamic
- Differencing

Fixed disks allocate their maximum storage at creation time. The size of a fixed disk stays the same all the time. Since all available storage is allocated at creation time, a fixed disk offers reliable and great performance.

Dynamic disks are created with just their header information and allocate more space when there is more data written to the disks. Due to their constant growth, the constant reclaiming of more storage and editing the metadata of the virtual disk, dynamic disks have a slight performance penalty over fixed disks. The recommendation in the past for production environments with Hyper-V clearly pointed to fixed disks. However, in the current version of Hyper-V, there are great improvements in this sector too. A dynamic disk is still slower than a fixed disk but the difference is much smaller today. There is a measurable performance hit of about 3 to 5 percent over a fixed disk in real-life scenarios. These little performance hits are not worth the management and cost downside of using fixed disks, in most customer situations. In my opinion, dynamic disks should be the default option for your workload, including production systems, unless the support requirements of your application demand otherwise. Keep in mind that Hyper-V supports thin provisioning of storage; combining this with dynamic disks allows you to have a very flexible management approach for Hyper-V disks.

Differencing disks use a parent/child-relation-based linked disk approach. A differencing disk is created and linked to a parent disk, typically containing a generalized sysprep image. A VM based on the child disk will then write all subsequent changes and customization like the child disk. These deployment scenarios are very fast and they are a great option for lab environments and VDI deployments. Differencing disks come with a high performance impact and a higher management complexity; therefore, they should not be used on production server deployments.

You can convert the disk type through PowerShell even while converting the disk format as well:

```
Convert-VHD -Path d:\VM01.vhd -DestinationPath d:\VM01.vhdx

-VHDType dynamic
```

There is a fourth disk type available in Hyper-V, a pass-through disk. Pass-through disks (raw) are not virtual hard disks. They directly use a physical volume without a virtualization container in between. In the past, this was a great way of achieving performance. In the recent Hyper-V versions, Pass-through disks have not offered advantages but several disadvantages such as limited mobility and manageability. Therefore, do not use pass-through disks anymore. Convert them by executing the following command:

```
New-VHD -Path "D:\VMS\Converted.VHDX" -Dynamic -SourceDisk 5
```

On the Hyper-V host where `Sourcedisk` adds the disk number from the host to convert, please note that the source disk must be offline for this operation.

Checkpoints

Formally called snapshots, checkpoints are a great way to create points in time of your VMs. Test updates and migrations with live exports or checkpoints of your VMs. Every time you create a checkpoint, a differencing disk will be created (avhdx) file. All changes occurring to this VM will be written to the new child disk. If you apply the checkpoint and jump back in time with your VM, the child disk will simply be deleted. If you delete the snapshot, the two disks are merged into a clean vhdx file. Since checkpoints use differencing disks, keep in mind that every checkpoint reduces the virtual machine performance slightly.

Besides the performance, checkpoints are hard to manage, and some tools and backup programs have issues with existing checkpoints. Checkpoints offer great flexibility; however, use them only if you really need to and delete them when you don't need them anymore.

Use the following command to create checkpoints:

```
Checkpoint-VM -Name Test -SnapshotName Snapshot1
```

There are some common best practices around checkpoints:

- The most important rule for checkpoints—use them as rarely as possible.
- Do not forget that checkpoints are no substitution for backups.
- Delete checkpoints as soon as possible.
- Never delete a checkpoint file on the file level. Delete checkpoints through Hyper-V only.
- Use snapshots with caution on domain controllers and other database servers. They have prerequirements stated in their system requirements.

Multipath I/O

When working with highly available storage systems, you do not only want the storage systems to avoid a single point of failure but also its connections. Therefore, it's best practice to have multiple connections between your storage infrastructure and your Hyper-V Server systems. Multipath I/O ensures that redundant paths between these systems are detected and the corresponding disks are only registered once. This is essential to ensure seamless disk management. With active MPIO, a path to your storage might get lost without any interruption to your virtual machines. SMB3 handles automatic MPIO, for all other storage architectures follow these steps to enable MPIO via PowerShell:

```
Enable-WindowsOptionalFeature –Online –FeatureName MultiPathIO
```

If you use iSCSI Storage, run the following command:

```
Enable-MSDSMAutomaticClaim -BusType iSCSI
```

If you use SAS storage, run the following command:

```
Enable-MSDSMAutomaticClaim -BusType SAS
```

To ensure a round-robin switching between the available paths, run the following command:

```
Set-MSDSMGlobalDefaultLoadBalancePolicy -Policy RR
```

It's best practice to set the disk time-out to 60 seconds as shown in the following command:

```
Set-MPIOSetting -NewDiskTimeout 60
```

These settings are valid for the default MPIO module of Windows Server 2012 R2 and provide optimal performance. If you are using vendor-specific storage DSMs, make sure you consult their documentation for optimal configuration. If you have storage DSMs supported by Hyper-V available from your storage vendor, you should prefer them over the default ones.

Cluster Shared Volumes

The most common question on **Cluster Shared Volumes (CSVs)** is how many you need and how huge they may get filled with data. As mentioned before, it's a good rule of thumb to create one CSV per Cluster node; in larger environments with more than eight cluster nodes, a CSV per-two-to-four nodes. The number of VMs per-CSV is not limited. Commonly, I do not see more than 50 VMs on a CSV for Server VMs and 100 VMs for Client VMs in the VDI environment. However, don't think in units here, plan in IOPS. Spread the IOPs evenly between your CSVs. To utilize the redundant storage hardware I wrote about earlier, never use a single CSV. Start with at least two CSVs to spread the load over your two storage controllers. This isn't necessarily a design of CSVs, rather a behavior of SAN and how it manages its disks. If you use one CSV, it's possible that SAN allocates "ownership" of that LUN to a single controller and could introduce a bottleneck in performance. Dividing the storage may allow the SAN to leverage an active-active configuration and potentially increase performance.

Metadata changes can only occur on the CSV coordinator, so make sure you use the CSV coordinator when applying changes such as expanding disks or moving files to the CSV. To identify the CSV coordinator, use the following cmdlet:

```
Get-ClusterSharedVolume
```

Also, identify the coordinator in the Node column. This cmdlet is also used to manage all relevant settings around CSVs. The coordinator is also known as the "owner node" in the Failover Cluster Manager console.

> CSVs can be renamed on the filesystem level (http://bit. ly/11A6nS7), as well as on the cluster object level (http:// bit.ly/1vxAUFF). This should be done prior to running any VMs from the CSV.

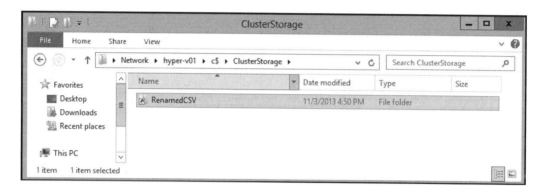

For optimal performance on CSVs, make sure that you defrag your virtual hard disks before moving them to a CSV by adding disk images to a VM, creating checkpoints and also the VM memory itself uses space on your CSVs. When a VM is powered on, it creates a file of size equal to the RAM in the VM folder on the CSV when the automatic stop action of the VM is on "save". Plan to fill up your CSVs with a maximum of 75 percent of its capacity to allow growth of all these files. If you want to know how much free space is available on your CSVs considering all dependencies, there is a great PowerShell script available on this page at http://bit.ly/1mloKQC.

Cluster Shared Volumes can be encrypted with Bitlocker; they will receive a performance hit around 20-30 percent. Encrypting your CSVs with Bitlocker not only increases the physical security of the data, it is also a great way to reduce the risk of data loss in a case of a hard disk change for whatever reason.

CSVs comes with special configuration considerations. Make sure the network adapters used for CSVs have the client for Microsoft networks and file and printer sharing for Microsoft networks is enabled. In most cases, it's suggested that you activate Microsoft Failover Cluster Virtual Adapter Performance Filter too. However, if you are using Guest Cluster in your virtual machine, this setting should be disabled on the host level to avoid problems with backups and cluster options.

Enabling the CSV cache provides caching at the block level for read-only, unbuffered I/O operations by allocating system memory (RAM) as cache. 80 percent of the physical RAM can be used as a CSV cache. It's best practice to use the CSV cache on Hyper-V Clusters. I've seen best performance/price ratios around 512-1024 MB; however, it should not be larger than 2 GB. Use the following command to configure the CSV cache in an elevated prompt to set the cache to 512 MB of data and use this value as a default for your CSV files:

```
(Get-Cluster).BlockCacheSize = 512
```

Data deduplication

Windows Server 2012 R2 with Hyper-V offers built-in deduplication at no extra charge. It's a great way to reduce your storage capacity footprint with very little configuration. However, data deduplication still comes at a price—it requires additional I/O capacity. Therefore, on a general use file server, it will not affect hot data until it's reached a certain file change age. Besides the I/O-hit, volumes with active deduplication will fragment more easily causing single file operations taking longer on deduped volumes. Hyper-V takes some precautions to avoid a big performance hit, that is, every block referenced more than 100 times will be written a second time. Real-life experiences tell us that the overall gains in saved space outweighs the performance cost on file servers, library servers, and VDI Hyper-V hosts. It is not supported to run Windows data deduplication on running VMs with server workloads. Before using deduplication, you can test how much space saving dedup will get you on a volume with the PowerShell command after dedup feature is enabled:

```
ddpeval.exe <Path>
```

Enable the `Dedup` feature by running the following cmdlet on the host level:

```
Install-windowsFeature FS-Data-Deduplication
```

Before using deduplication, you can test how much space saving Dedup will get you on a volume with the following command after the Dedup feature is enabled:

```
Dedup is enabled on a per Volume Base:
```

```
Enable-DeDupVolume D:
```

Configure the file age needed for deduplication to occur. This directly affects the necessary storage-IOPS:

```
Set-DedupVolume -Volume D: -MinimumFileAgeDays 5
```

Start a Dedup job on a specified volume:

```
Start-DedupJob D: -Type Optimization
```

To create a regular Dedup-Schedule that will deduplicate the drive in a 10-hour window per week, use the following command:

```
New-dedupschedule -Name "Elanity-Dedup01" -Type Optimization -Days Sat,
Wed -Start 23:00 -DurationHours 10
```

Keep in mind that data deduplication is not supported on system and boot volumes. That's another reason why it's a good idea to move your data to a second volume. The volume must be local, as data deduplication is not possible on removable or mapped drives.

If you already have deduplication enabled on your storage platform beneath Hyper-V, leave it there. It's more efficient to run this on the hardware/storage level. There is also a small additional storage saving by running Dedup on hardware and software level simultaneously. However, the downsides such as more resource utilization overweigh, so activate Dedup only on one level.

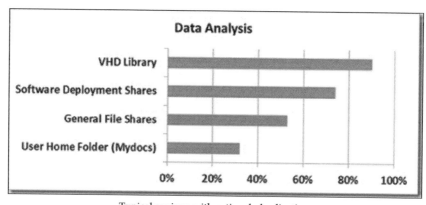

Typical savings with active deduplication

If you are using a Virtual desktop infrastructure running on Hyper-V, you have hit the unique condition where it's supported to deduplicate live data. To enable deduplication of your running client VMs to ensure huge data savings, run the following command:

```
Enable-DedupVolume C:\ClusterStorage\Volume1 –UsageType HyperV
```

Keep in mind that data deduplication is a postprocessing job, so be sure there is enough storage capacity available for new data until it gets shrinked by Dedup.

Storage Quality of Service

Windows Server with Hyper-V offers great **Quality of Service (QoS)** features to separate hardware resources between different virtual machines and services ensuring a full isolation. Since earlier versions, this is available for compute resources, RAM, and networking. With Windows Server 2012 R2, these capabilities are added for storage as well on a per virtual disk level for VHDX files. This is a great feature to ensure that a single malfunctioning VM on a huge CSV does not affect any other workload.

Storage QoS is specified in 8 KB-block IOPS. There are two types of storage QoS settings available in Hyper-V:

- **Minimum**: This allows you to set a minimal I/O threshold. However, this cannot guarantee a minimum amount of available I/O performance to a virtual disk and this cannot be controlled by Hyper-V. The settings just trigger a hard-to-read notification if the minimal value is not reached by the VM. Typically, there is no need to specify this setting as long as you are monitoring your storage infrastructure.

- **Maximum**: This allows you to specify the maximum IOPS allowed for a virtual hard disk that is associated with a virtual machine. This is a powerful value and should be used on all data disks of your VMs. However, use high enough values to provide a flexible performance structure. This setting prevents malfunctions without limiting the flexibility gained by virtualization.

A great way to determine the used IOPS of a VM is VMResourceMetering. A guide on how to use this can be found at `http://bit.ly/1lUjK4q`.

Storage QoS is enabled the moment you activate the Hyper-V role. configure it with the following command:

```
Set-VMHardDiskDrive -VMName EYVM01 -Path .\EYVM01Data.vhdx

-MaximumIOPS 5000 -MinimumIOPS 100
```

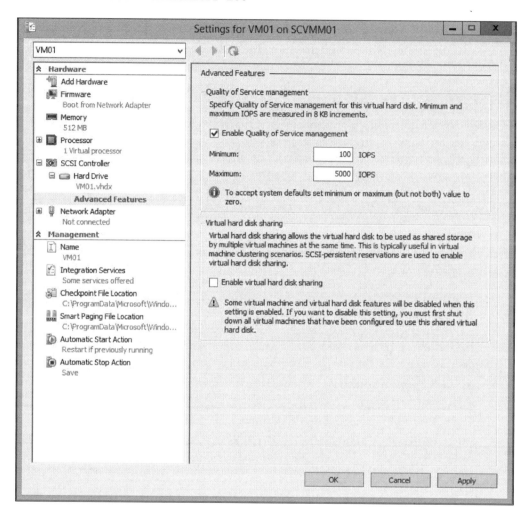

NTFS versus Resilient File System

Hyper-V supports two filesystems, the classic NTFS, and the more recent **Resilient File-System (ReFS)**. ReFS is a great filesystem—for a later date. Currently, it lacks some key capabilities such as deduplication. It is supported on CSVs, but most backup applications have problems with it. It is best practice to stick with NTFS for Hyper-V and take a look at ReFS with a later version. When using NTFS with Hyper-V, it's best practice to format the volume with 64 KB block size for optimal performance. The partition alignment is handled automatically, so you don't have to worry about it in recent Hyper-V versions.

However, if you want to use ReFS, it is a great filesystem to host image libraries on a separate volume of your file server.

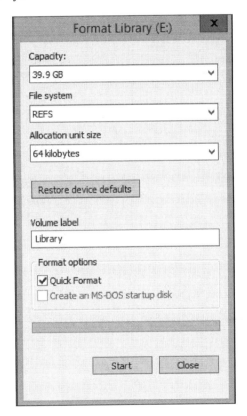

The iSCSI target

Microsoft Windows Server includes an iSCSI target to provide iSCSI LUNs from Windows Server software instead of an iSCSI SAN. This enables you to provide central storage with whatever storage is attached to the server running the iSCSI target. The iSCSI target is supported for production. However, though there is a a performance penalty against native iSCSI SAN systems, they are preferred for lab and demonstration purposes.

An iSCSI target should run on a dedicated machine and never on a Hyper-V host or another production workload-hosting server. Use PowerShell to create and configure a iSCSI target. Activate the necessary features using the following command lines:

```
Add-WindowsFeature -Name FS-iSCSITarget-Server

Add-WindowsFeature -Name iSCSITarget-VSS-VDS
```

Create a new LUN:

```
New-IscsiVirtualDisk -Path d:\VHD\LUN1.vhdx -Size 60GB
```

Create a new iSCSI target:

```
New-IscsiServerTarget -TargetName Target1 -InitiatorId IPAddress:192.168.
1.240,IPAddress:192.168.1.241
```

Assign the iSCSI LUN to its target:

```
Add-IscsiVirtualDiskTargetMapping -TargetName target1 Path d:\VHD\LUN1.
vhdx -Lun 10
```

Connect to your iSCSI target through the iSCSI iniator on your Hyper-V hosts:

```
Connect-IscsiTarget -NodeAddress <targetIQN>
```

You have the option to connect to the target from within the VMs and not from the Hyper-V hosts. This option comes with a slightly negative performance impact and additional points of administration for your storage infrastructure.

Summary

After completing this chapter, you are now aware of the most common storage architectures for Hyper-V. You learned about the technologies used behind it and their best practice configurations.

Now, continue to *Chapter 5, Network Best Practices*, to learn about networking. If you want to learn even more about storage, there are some additional tuning tips in *Chapter 6, Hyper-V Performance Tuning*.

5

Network Best Practices

"In networking assumptions can be deadly, so while you may trust your designs, you absolutely need to verify them, learn their behavior under normal operating conditions and during failover to make sure the solutions works as designed."

Didier van Hoye – MVP Hyper-V

This chapter will make you familiar with the common network architectures compatible with Hyper-V and how to use them more efficiently. A complete network virtualization solution was introduced by Windows Server 2012 and offers a huge variety of networking options for Hyper-V. **Software-defined networking (SDN)** allows you to design your network independently from the physical network topology.

In this chapter, you will learn about the following topics:

- Virtual switches, vNICS, tNICS
- NIC Teaming
- Creating virtual networks
- Software-defined networking
- **IP address management (IPAM)**

Networking overview

Hyper-V Network Virtualization provides an abstraction layer above your physical network very similar to how server virtualization provides VMs from a physical host. Network virtualization decouples virtual networks from the physical network infrastructure and removes the constraints of physical adapters, VLAN, and segregated networks on a physical level. Hyper-V Network Virtualization is a big prerequisite for real flexibility in an IT infrastructure. An elastic IT infrastructure, commonly named Cloud, benefits from this feature and allows efficient management of networking.

In the past, the necessary multitenant isolation while fulfilling all security requirements could only be achieved through huge investments in network infrastructure. Windows Server 2012 R2 with Hyper-V changed that. Its dynamic and flexible network approach allows you to reach this target with less physical networking hardware but increased flexibility. The abstraction is reached by using the Hyper-V virtual switch, which is explained in the next paragraphs. Virtual machines use **virtual network interfaces (VIF)** that communicate through a VMBUS to the virtual switch. This complete stack is controlled by the Hyper-V root partition, also called management OS and the vNICs of the virtual machines.

All network-related settings in this chapter will be configured via PowerShell directly at the operating system level. This configuration can also be achieved through **System Center Virtual Machine Manager (SCVMM)**, about which you will learn more in *Chapter 7, Management with System Center*. As a rule of thumb, if you are planning to use more than three Hyper-V Hosts, the use of SCVMM is recommended and the network configuration should originate from SCVMM. It is not possible to manage network settings via SCVMM that were created by Hyper-V PowerShell.

Windows Server 2012 and Windows Server 2012 R2 support converged networking, where different types of network traffic share the same Ethernet network infrastructure. With features such as **Quality of Service (QoS)**, we are enabled to consolidate network traffic on fewer physical adapters. Combined with traffic isolation methods such as VLANs, you can isolate and control the network traffic completely independent of the physical design.

Let's go into the details of Hyper-V network's best practices.

The Virtual Switch

The Hyper-V Virtual Switch is a software-based layer-2 network switch that is available in Hyper-V Manager when you add the Hyper-V Server role. The switch allows us to connect virtual machines to both virtual networks and the physical network. In addition, the Hyper-V Virtual Switch provides policy enforcement for security, isolation, and service levels, and can be extended for advanced management purposes such as anti-virus or diagnostic additions. You can even extend the default Hyper-V Switch with the well-known Cisco Switch Nexus 1000V. If you are already using Cisco Network Infrastructure, you should use this extension and manage the Cisco Nexus 1000V with your existing Cisco Management infrastructure.

Little known fact

There is a free version of this switch extension with essential networking features available at `http://bit.ly/1mYS9jW`. The advanced edition adds only security features known from the Nexus switching series.

The following diagram shows Hyper-V virtual switch and extensions:

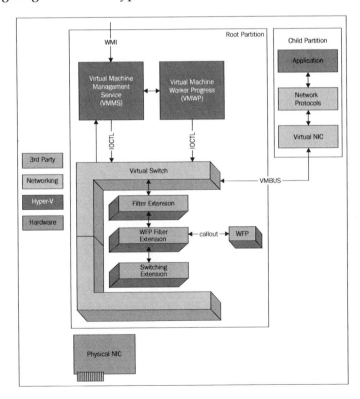

There are three types of Hyper-V Virtual Switches available in Hyper-V. It's important to know in which situation each type is best used.

The external vSwitch

The external vSwitch is bound to a physical network card in your Hyper-V host or on its abstraction layers, such as a logical teaming interface. VMs connected to this switch are able to communicate with network devices outside the Hyper-V hosts, that is, clients accessing VMs.

In *Chapter 1, Accelerate Hyper-V Deployment,* we already used PowerShell to create an external vSwitch:

```
New-VMSwitch -Name external -NetAdapterName "Local Area Connection 2"
```

For internal and private vSwitches, which I am going to introduce, the `NetAdapterName` parameter isn't available since no external adapter is used. You also used the parameter `-AllowManagementOS $true` earlier, which allows the same physical network adapter to be used for a virtual switch as well as for connecting to your Hyper-V hosts. This shared setup should only be used when you do not have enough physical adapters available and are not using **converged networking**—a concept I will introduce later in this chapter. Other than that, this is not a preferred configuration from a performance point of view.

The internal vSwitch

The internal vSwitch is used for communication between virtual machines on the same host as well as communication to the Hyper-V host itself. It does not allow for external communication. This is used for isolated lab environments that involve the Hyper-V host, for example, accessing different VMs from the Hyper-V host.

To create an internal vSwitch, use the following cmdlet run from an elevated shell:

```
New-VMSwitch -Name internal -SwitchType internal -Notes 'Internal VMs
only'
```

The private vSwitch

The private vSwitch allows for communication between Hyper-V virtual machines on the same host. It does not allow for external communication or communication with the host itself. This is mainly used for **guest cluster networking** as described in *Chapter 2, High Availability Scenarios,* as well as for lab purposes.

To create a private vSwitch, use the following cmdlet run from an elevated shell:

```
New-VMSwitch -Name private -SwitchType Private
```

Hyper-V networking is capable of using VLANs; however, they are not configured on a vSwitch level, but on a virtual interface level. The VLAN ID checkbox in the Virtual Switch Manager is only intended for setting a host OS VLAN when using the `AllowManagementOS` parameter.

The virtual interface

Hyper-V offers two types of network adapters: the **legacy network adapter** and the default **synthetic network adapter**. The legacy adapter was primarily used for PXE Boot capabilities. However, with only 100 Mb of network bandwidth, it should be avoided. On generation 2 VMs, the legacy network adapter is no longer available and a PXE Boot is possible with the default network adapter there.

A network adapter is always connected to a vSwitch, which was described earlier in this chapter. After connecting the vmNIC to a vSwitch, we can now add this particular NIC to a specific VLAN. All network traffic to and from this VM will go through this VLAN (tagged). Instead of adding 15 different Ethernet cables to your Hyper-V host when using 15 different networks for your systems, it is a great option to enable VLAN trunking and communicate with just 1-2 physical NICs.

To add a single VLAN to our vNIC external via PowerShell, use:

```
Set-VMNetworkAdapterVlan -VMName EyVM01 -VMNetworkAdapterName "External"
-Access -VlanId 10
```

Little known fact

It is also possible to add VLAN ranges to a vNIC via trunking:

```
Set-VMNetworkAdapterVlan -VMName EYVM01-Trunk
-AllowedVlanIdList 1-100 -NativeVlanId 10
```

All the tagged traffic for VLANs 1-100 will be allowed to and from the VM. The untagged traffic will be defaulted to VLAN 10.

There are also additional capabilities for Hyper-V and VLANs, such as using VLAN isolation modes and promiscuous modes for more advanced scenarios with dedicated isolation and sharing requirements between VLANs (`http://bit.ly/1mDy6GH`).

It's best practice to stick to just one VLAN per NIC until you cannot fulfill your requirements with it. If you need to use trunking or other special scenarios, it is highly recommended that you use SCVMM for VLAN Management. See *Chapter 7, Management with System Center*, for more details.

After enabling VLANs on our vNICs, we share a single or a few physical connections between these VLANs. To make sure our backup network is not using all the available bandwidth and impacting the production VMs, we use bandwidth management for our virtual interfaces, also known as **Quality of Service (QoS)**. QoS allows us to meet the service requirements of a service or an application by measuring the network bandwidth, detecting bandwidth limits, and prioritizing—or throttling—network traffic via policies. Hyper-V gives us the possibility to manage two QoS settings for networking:

- Minimum bandwidth
- Maximum bandwidth

These settings are provided on absolute bandwidth and are inflexible to hardware changes. It's best practice to set a minimum bandwidth, but don't restrict the maximum bandwidth. To set bandwidth limits leveraging this approach, use the following PowerShell cmdlet:

```
Set-VMNetworkAdapter -VMName EYVM1 -MinimumBandwidth 1000000
```

The absolute bandwidth is provided in bits per second and will be rounded to a byte. The settings will be reflected in the GUI:

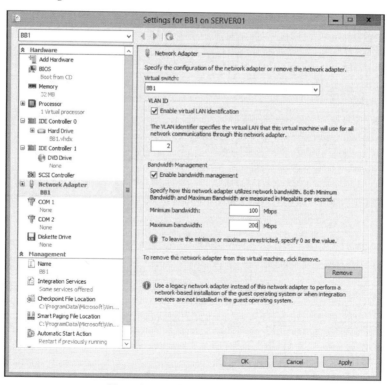

Hyper-V virtual interface properties

In this example, I've also set the maximum bandwidth to 200 Mbps.

However, there is a far better approach using relative weights instead of absolute values. These values are not reflected in the GUI, so PowerShell is our friend again. To enable the use of weights, we first enable the vSwitch for relative weight and then set a default value to our created vSwitch:

1. Create a vSwitch with the `DefaultFlowMinimumBandwidthWeight` parameter:

   ```
   New-VMSwitch -Name external -NetAdapterName "Local Area Connection
   2" -DefaultFlowMinimumBandwidthWeight
   ```

2. Set the external VMSwitch, `DefaultFlowMinimumBandwidthWeight` as 50. This weight will be assigned to all the adapters on the vSwitch without a specific weight, set a higher weight (upto 100) for more important services, and less weight for less important services.

On a typical Hyper-V cluster, the following networks are available and I have attached my best practice bandwidth QoS configuration:

Network	QoS minimum weight
Management	10
Cluster	15
Live migration	25
Virtual machines	50

These networks and their weights are best placed on a NIC Team for redundancy.

NIC Teaming

Before Windows Server 2012, the teaming of Network Interface Cards was a part of the NIC-driver but not of the operating system. This policy led to regular support cases with problematic implementations, and today's NIC Teaming is done on operating system level. NIC Teaming in Windows Server 2012 R2 allows us to span a team over NICs from different vendors and of different bandwidths with classic **Load Balancing and Failover (LBFO)** capabilities. However, it's best practice to have only active interfaces with equal bandwidth active in one team. Creating a NIC Team will create a logical network object, a **team NIC (tNIC)**, that then is connected to our created Hyper-V vSwitch.

It's possible to create additional tNICs on an existing team without using vSwitches. However, this option lacks the ability of QoS and should be avoided.

There are different Teaming modes available in Windows Server 2012 R2:

- **Switch independent**: This should be your default option for newly created teams. It does not involve any configuration on involved physical switches that are connected to the teamed NICs. It's also the "must have" setting when the NICs of your team are connected to redundant switches, which are highly recommended.

- **Static Teaming**: To use static Teaming, all NICs of your team must be connected to the same switch or support **Multi-Chassis Link Aggregation**. The used switch ports must be configured for static/general Teaming.

- **LACP**: To use LACP, all the NICs of your team must be connected to the same switch or support Multi-Chassis Link Aggregation. LACP allows a semi-automatic configuration of the connected switch, preferable over static Teaming.

There are three different load balancing modes available, which define how the traffic is spread among the team members:

- **Address hashing**: This creates hashes for outgoing network packets. Every packet with the same hash will be routed to the same network adapter. Incoming traffic is spread by the switch with switch-dependent configurations, but will use only the first NIC in the team for switch-independent configurations.

- **Hyper-V port**: This spreads the load based on the vSwitch port assignments. Single NIC-VMs will not spread their load over different network adapters, but all adapters are used for spreading all outgoing VM traffic. The same interface as the outgoing packet will be used for incoming traffic for this specific VM and not be spread over multiple adapters.

- **Dynamic**: This combines the Hyper-V port receiving the algorithm with the dynamic optimization of address hashing for outgoing packets. A sorting algorithm will optimize the hash table for more load balancing. With Windows Server 2012 R2, this leads to an effective and balanced distribution of the outbound and inbound traffic.

Let's see which combinations are ready for real-world scenarios:

- **Switch-independent configuration / Dynamic distribution**: This mode is best used for Teaming in both native and Hyper-V environments, except for guest-VM Teaming. It offers the best performance with failover capabilities.

- **Switch-independent configuration / Address hash distribution**: This mode is best used for guest-VM Teaming. Creating a team inside a VM allows the VM to be connected to more than one vSwitch. This is a typical setup in SR-IOV setups (See *Chapter 6, Hyper-V Performance Tuning*, for details).

There is also an option to specify a standby adapter that's passive until one adapter fails. It's best practice to use all the available NICs in active teams.

Switch-dependent policies are more complex and do not provide better performance in my experience.

For more details, refer to the Windows Server 2012 R2 NIC Teaming user guide at `http://bit.ly/UdlvMh`.

The following screenshot shows the Hyper-V Teaming properties:

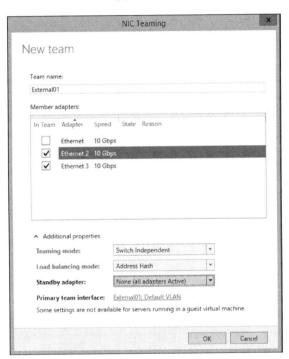

Converged networking

With Hyper-V Network Virtualization — VLANs, QoS, and NIC — we now have great tools at hand for creating true software-defined networking, independent of the underlying physical hardware. This enables us to implement the network design of our choice without the need for additional physical NICs. Use a few high-speed NICs instead of many single Gigabit NICs. Team those NICs and add a converged networking solution on it. Use the virtual NICs on a vSwitch (instead of tNICs without a vSwitch) to add QoS configurations. This offers many possibilities and there are no right or wrong options here. I'm introducing a converged network design that I have often implemented myself, and also regularly found in production environments.

A switch-independent/dynamic team is created on all available NICs of the fastest bandwidth, which are not used for guest-OS clusters. A dynamic switch is created above the team. Four vNICs will be created on the management OS and bound to the created vSwitch via PowerShell:

```
Add-VMNetworkAdapter -ManagementOS -Name "Management" -SwitchName
"External" MinimumBandwidthWeight 10
```

```
Add-VMNetworkAdapter -ManagementOS -Name "Live Migration" -SwitchName
"External" MinimumBandwidthWeight 25
```

```
Add-VMNetworkAdapter -ManagementOS -Name "VMs" -SwitchName "External"
MinimumBandwidthWeight 50
```

```
Add-VMNetworkAdapter -ManagementOS -Name "Cluster" -SwitchName "External"
MinimumBandwidthWeight 15
```

The result will be a very flexible networking solution fulfilling all our Hyper-V requirements for production workloads. The following screenshot shows a converged network:

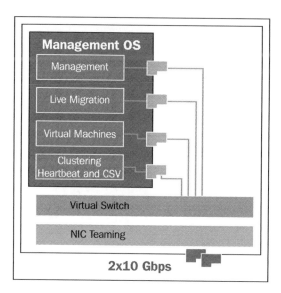

It's highly recommended to use a converged architecture instead of a classical physical mapping of networks.

Storage network

If you are using **Fibre Channel Infrastructure** for storage communication, you don't need additional considerations to integrate this communication into your converged network. However, if you are using the iSCSI communication, it's highly recommended to use another network for storage communication. The iSCSI communication uses MPIO for resiliency instead of network Teaming. There is just one upcoming scenario where iSCSI over teamed interfaces is possible, in all the major scenarios teaming iSCSI communication is not supported. Visit `http://bit.ly/1mVYDyq` for more details.

It's best practice to separate the iSCSI communication from other traffic on a host level, so use two dedicated network cards on the host. Don't add them to a team, instead use the MPIO feature for resiliency.

If you are using SMB3 communication for your storage, don't integrate the communication into your network team, use the dedicated RDMA interfaces for SMB Direct communication for this workload.

SMB Direct

When using SMB3 storage communication or Live Migration, it is not possible to utilize optimal performance through our existing converged networking design. In this case, it's highly recommended to use RDMA-capable network cards. Add two network cards with RDMA capability to your hosts. Do not team them. Do not use MPIO on them. Configure both to use different subnets, Windows Server will automatically spread the workload between the NICs using SMB multichannel. RDMA enables high-performance networking while using very little CPU load. SMB Direct will be automatically enabled when RDMA-capable NICs are detected on the host.

There are three types of RDMA-aware network architectures available:

- **ROCE: ROCE** stands for **RDMA over converged Ethernet** and utilizes existing Ethernet network switches. It is complex to implement and as of today, it is not routable by design. For details and implementation guidelines, visit `http://bit.ly/1miEA97`.

- **iWARP**: iWARP uses a connection-oriented transport instead of the link-based ROCE. It is way more easy to implement and to maintain in my experience, but still, Ethernet utilizes existing Ethernet network switches. There are far less support calls per implementation from customers using iWARP over ROCE. It is a routable protocol; so, you can use it across data centers. For details and implementation guidelines, visit `http://bit.ly/1ebTrCc`.

- **InfiniBand**: InfiniBand uses its own network architecture and does not leverage existing Ethernet infrastructure. It offers great performance and huge bandwidths for a significant entry price. InfiniBand is your choice if you want performance without trade-offs. For details and implementation guidelines, visit `http://bit.ly/1tTe7IK`.

All three types of these architectures have the ability to provide great performance for SMB storage communication and Live Migration. It is not necessary, in my experience, to use RDMA capabilities if you are not using 10 GB Ethernet or greater bandwidths for VM networking.

Advanced networking options

After configuring our converged fabric, it's now time to take a look at more advanced networking configuration options in Hyper-V. To take the level of network virtualization even further, it's possible to run virtual machines with the same IP addresses on the same network without causing conflicts. The techniques used behind this are mainly NVGRE for encapsulation and an NVGRE gateway for outside communication. These are great options, but not commonly needed. Stay away from these settings until you really need to use them. Since uncommon options are not the focus of this book, visit `http://bit.ly/Ud5WXq` for details.

A far more common option is the use of **DHCP Guard**. Having a Roque DHCP Server on the network can very quickly become a very ugly problem for nearly every production environment. A Windows DHCP Server in an **Active Directory Domain** must be authorized until it starts broadcasting DHCP offers. In other topologies, nothing else is stopping Roque DHCP Servers. Hyper-V can protect you from unsolicited router and DHCP Server offers at a network level.

It's best practice to enable DHCP Guard for all VMs and disable it for particular VMs where these services are needed. Of course, we use PowerShell for this task:

```
Get-VM | Set-VMNetworkAdapter -DhcpGuard On
```

This is not enabled by default, since there is a minimal performance impact for filtering out unsolicited DHCP packets at a network level. In my experience, this performance hit is virtually unmeasureable.

There is a similar service called **Router Guard** for filtering ICMP Router Advertisements and redirect messages, but the use of Router Guard is very uncommon.

IPAM

One of my most favorite features in Windows Server 2012 R2 is the **IP address management (IPAM)** module. It's very simple and quick to use, but also very effective.

When you need a static IP address for a newly created virtual machine, where do you obtain it? Ping a random address and see whether it times out? Check the DNS server for records? Check the DHCP leases and reservations or an outdated Excel file? All of these are common processes, but there is still a chance for failure and to use those IP addresses already in use.

IPAM offers a dynamic version of the Excel list. It periodically scans your DNS and DHCP Servers to document all the taken IP addresses and offer the next *real free* IP address that you can use for your new VM, and have it documented automatically.

I do not know of a way to configure IPAM completely through PowerShell, so I recommend that you follow this guide instead (`http://bit.ly/1qgEw1R`):

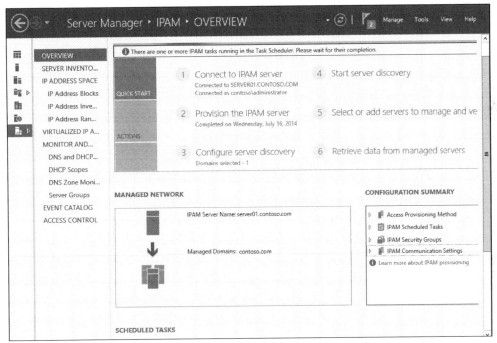

IPAM

Summary

After completing this chapter, you should now be familiar with best practice options to configure a basic Hyper-V network, utilizing the potential of converged networking.

Now, continue to *Chapter 6, Hyper-V Performance Tuning*, for more advanced configurations focusing on deploying the most effective production systems. There are additional networking tuning options using hardware accelerating features in this chapter.

6

Hyper-V Performance Tuning

"Guesswork is the path to failure. Start on a good footing with MAP and know your requirements. Follow the best practices of this book to avoid most performance issues. And practice monitoring your hosts and workloads so you can quickly fix issues if they happen."

Aidan Finn – MVP Hyper-V

After completing the basic configuration of all Hyper-V components, it's now time for additional performance tuning.

These are the topics that we will cover in this chapter:

- Measuring performance
- Performance tuning and sizing guidelines for:
    - Hardware
    - Storage/network
    - Hyper-V server role
- Benchmarking
- Tuning for client virtualization and virtual GPUs

Measuring performance

Before we start getting into performance tuning, it's necessary to have an understanding of the current situation. Many sizings for Hyper-V setups, have seemingly been based on some random goodwill rough estimates without recognizing the current situation or future requirements. A far better approach to size Hyper-V setups relies on using the free MAP Toolkit, which you've already seen in *Chapter 1, Accelerate Hyper-V Deployment*. MAP collects performance counters of all the relevant components for a Hyper-V setup. In the same way as it is used to determine your Hyper-V sizing, it can be also used to create a performance baseline of your Hyper-V setup. This can also be achieved using Microsoft **System Center Operations Manager**. If you already have SCOM in place, this tool should be preferred over MAP. See *Chapter 7, Management with System Center* for details.

Both tools continuously read performance counters from Hyper-V hosts and their VMs and archive them in a database. Run these tasks for a continuous time, I recommend a full month, to establish an adequate baseline. In this time, you will collect the minimum, maximum, and average performance counters of your systems. The minimum values give you no real sizing information; however, the average value delivers great information for basic sizing, and the maximum values allow you to factor in the peak performance of the systems. The following screenshot is a summary of the performance:

Operating System	CPU	Cores	Average CPU Utilization (%)	Maximum CPU Utilization (%)	95th Percentile CPU Utilizati	Memory (MB)	Average Memory
Microsoft(R) Windows(R)	Intel(R) Xeon(R) CPU X5660	Insufficient	0,9	6,42	2,05	2048	0,65
Microsoft Windows	Intel(R) Xeon(R) CPU X5660	1	0,16	8,88	0,45	4096	0,55
Microsoft Windows XP	Intel(R) Xeon(R) CPU X5660	1	3,98	10,34	7,95	2040	0,52
Microsoft Windows	Intel(R) Xeon(R) CPU E5-2630 0 @	4	5,06	30,02	18,36	51197	43,45
Microsoft Windows	Intel(R) Xeon(R) CPU X5660	4	2,81	18,32	5,2	24576	11,96
Microsoft Windows Server 2008 R2	Intel(R) Xeon(R) CPU X5660 @ 2.80GHz, 64 bit	4	5,02	42,37	12,48	16384	8,33

A real value can also be drawn from the 95-percentile values for CPU, RAM, disk, and networking performance counter to plan for a solid baseline. The 95 percentiles have been proven to be a reliable source for performance measurement and sizing.

The same performance counter used by the MAP Toolkit and SCOM to create these reports can be manually tracked and tuned using **Windows Performance Monitor (perfmon.exe)**.

The performance counter

Let's have a look at the most important performance counters for Hyper-V;
you can easily access them from **perfmon.exe**.

The following basic counters are important at the host level until otherwise
noted, but most of them can be used at the VM level as well.

Disk performance

Having enough capacity on your storage is important, but as we saw earlier, storage
in a data center is all about IOPs. There are two important performance counters
telling us that there are not enough IOPs available: \Logical Disk(*)\Avg. sec/
Read and \Logical Disk(*)\Avg. sec/Write.

They measure the disk latency of the systems following a shortage of IOPs. If the
storage subsystem provides enough IOPs, the latencies for read and write storage
performance should not go beyond 15 milliseconds.

A disk latency between 15 and 25 milliseconds, or even higher, can cause a
negative impact on the performance of your virtual machines and applications,
and a disk latency over 25 milliseconds will cause a negative impact for sure.
High disk latency is the number one reason for slow Hyper-V performance,
because a design for storage IOPs is often neglected.

Use the individual disk counter to filter this setting to a specific disk level.
Be aware while using logical disks from a SAN or NAS; this counter only
leverages the whole logical disk and not the individual physical disks.

Memory performance

To check whether enough memory is available inside a VM or at the Hyper-V
host level, use the following two performance counters:

- **\Memory\Available Mbytes**: This measures the RAM available for
  running the active processes. Make sure that at least 15 percent of the
  maximum installed memory is available. If this is not the case, add more
  RAM to the physical host or virtual machine. If you use dynamic memory
  inside a virtual machine, make sure that you increase the buffer to make
  more RAM available to the virtual machine.

- **\Memory\Pages/sec**: This counter measures the rate of how often the disk
  is accessed to resolve hard page faults. To achieve this, the operating system
  swaps the contents of memory to the disks, which affects the performance
  notably. Make sure that this counter stays below 500 pages per second;
  otherwise, this is a clear indicator that your system needs more RAM.

Network performance

Again, here are the two most important performance counters to measure the Hyper-V network performance:

- **\Network Interface(*)\Bytes Total/sec**: This counter measures the amount of current network utilization. Subtract this from the total network bandwidth available, and make sure that you get at least 20 percent of the remaining network bandwidth available.

- **\Network Interface(*)\Output Queue Length**: This counter measures the latency in sending network packets in the form of threads that wait on the NIC. This queue should always be zero; a value higher than 1 is a sign of degraded network performance.

To measure the network utilization on the guest operating systems, use the **\Hyper-V Virtual Network Adapter(*)\Bytes/sec** counter to identify which virtual network adapters are consuming the most network utilization.

Processor performance

Last but not least, here are the two top performance counters to measure the CPU performance at the host level:

- **\Processor(*)\% Processor Time**: This counter is applicable at the host level only and measures the overall CPU utilization. This counter should not exceed 80 percent in a good performance baseline.

- **\Hyper-V Hypervisor Logical Processor(_Total)\% Total Run Time**: This counter is used at the host level to evaluate a guest operating system processor.

To identify the CPU power used by the host itself, use the **Hyper-V Hypervisor Root Virtual Processor - % Total Run Time** counter.

You already learned about the **\Hyper-V Hypervisor Logical Processor(_Total)\% Total Run Time** counter at the host level. There is another counter that is very similar to this one: **Hyper-V Hypervisor Virtual Processor(_Total)\% Total Run Time**.

It is also run at the host level, but it leverages the amount of virtual processors you gave to each virtual machine and not the leveraged logical processors at the host level. This allows you to receive valuable sizing information. If the logical processor counter is high but the virtual processor counter is low, it means that you have allocated more vCPUs to VMs than physically available.

The **\Hyper-V Hypervisor Virtual Processor(*)\%Guest Run Time** counter allows
you to identify which vCPUs are consuming the logical CPU resources to find a
suitable candidate for deallocation. The following screenshot shows us how to
the performance counters with **Perfmon**:

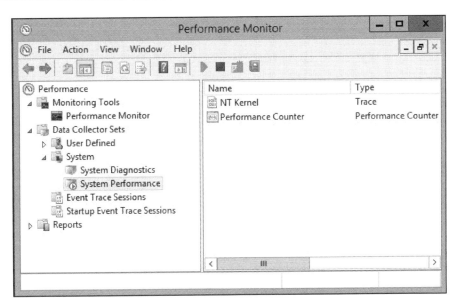

Performance tuning

After establishing performance-counter baselines, it's time to interpret them. The
values of networking, disks, and memory are self-explanatory, so let's go into the
details of CPU sizing.

If the logical processor counter is low, but the virtual processor counter is high,
it means that you can add more vCPUs to your virtual machines, as the logical
processors are still available.

Theoretically, there is really no upper limit to how many virtual CPUs you can
assign to virtual machines. The Microsoft recommendation is to not exceed more
than 8 virtual CPUs per physical CPU core for server workloads and more than
12 virtual CPUs per physical CPU core for VDI workloads. However, there is no
support limit, and there are low-workload scenarios where this recommendation
can be extended.

My real-world experience from working with performance counters and baselines
is to use a 1:4 ratio for production workloads as a rule of thumb and a 1:12 ratio
for Test/VDI workloads as a sizing baseline.

Keep in mind that a virtual machine with four vCPUs can actually be slower than the same VM with only two vCPUs, because waiting for four available threads on the host can take longer than waiting for two available threads. That's why you should attach only necessary vCPUs to virtual machines and also avoid over commitment at the guest level.

Hyper-V power options and green IT

Windows Server with Hyper-V is optimized for performance as well as for green IT in the default configuration. Achieving both the targets at the same time is a trade-off. It is a trade-off for using nearly the best performance when needed, while saving as much power as possible. Hyper-V supports a lot of power-saving options, such as CPU core parking or changing processor speeds, but not all of them. The standby mode and hibernation are not possible on a Hyper-V host. I recommend a green-IT approach. About two-thirds of all the costs of a server in its typical life span are generated from operating costs such as cooling and the power of the system, and only one-third falls back on the initial costs of the server hardware itself. So, saving power is a very important factor when running IT infrastructures.

I have seen Hyper-V losing some benchmarks against other virtualization products, and on rare occasions, I have experienced performance trade-offs due to this green-IT-oriented behavior.

By teasing out the last few performance points of Hyper-V, but not caring about saving energy, it is possible to change this default behavior positioned on the power options of Hyper-V hosts.

A Windows Server installation, either at a physical or virtual level, will use the balanced power scheme by default. After switching this performance plan to high performance, I have seen better performance and lower latency on Hyper-V hosts with up to 10 percent difference. At the guest OS level (where a change in the power options does not have an effect), I have seen SQL databases perform up to 20 percent better when the underlying host uses the high-performance power plan.

I recommend that you use the following best practices:

- Leave the lab-utilized, test-utilized, and low-utilized Hyper-V hosts on the default *balanced* power plan
- Switch the power plan on typical utilized production hosts to *high performance*
- Leave the guest VM power plan on *balanced*

Also, when running benchmarks against "the other guys", make sure that you have the host power setting on high performance.

Change the power plan on the Hyper-V host to high performance by starting an elevated shell, and run the following command:

```
POWERCFG.EXE /S SCHEME_MIN
```

Don't get confused; SCHEME_MIN does not refer to minimum performance but to minimum power saving. It has the CPU turbo frequencies always enabled and disables core parking.

After that, the GUI will represent the setting, as shown in the following screenshot:

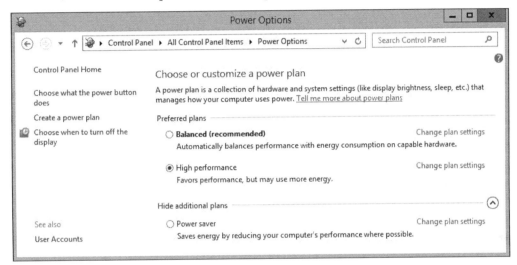

To revert to the balanced power scheme, use POWERCFG.EXE /S SCHEME_BALANCED.

Whatever power plan you use, make sure that you use high-efficiency power supplies and fans of variable speed in your servers to save as much energy and money as possible.

Hardware-tuning options

There are several options available to get more performance out of your Hyper-V hosts, starting with hardware features and going over hypervisor and driver configurations up to application tuning and usage scenarios. Let's start with the hardware options by selecting high-performance hardware for our Hyper-V host.

Adding more CPUs and cores as well as selecting processors with Hyper-V threading benefits the VM ratio that our host can handle. Choosing CPUs with bigger caches improves the overall Hyper-V performance. As of early 2014, Intel offers CPUs with 37, 5 MB smart cache, but they are nearly 7,000 USD far away from being as cheap as Intel's mainstream CPUs for virtualization.

Using CPUs with **Second Level Address Translation (SLAT)** is not required for server operating systems (for client operating systems, it is!) but is highly recommended. SLAT is also required for VDI workloads. Adding SLAT options such as **Extended Page Tables (EPT)** or **Nested Page Tables (NPT)** increases the overall Hyper-V performance. To take it further, choose CPUs with a higher frequency. Intel's Xeon E7v2 CPUs deliver up to 3.4 GHz frequency with the option to auto-increase up to 3.7 GHz per core. A core with doubled frequency typically provides better performance over two cores with a single frequency. Multiple cores do not provide a perfect scaling; they provide lesser scaling if hyper-threading is enabled, because hyper-threading relies on sharing resources of the same physical core.

There are only two supported CPU vendors for Hyper-V hosts as of today: Intel and AMD. I have tested both and was unable to detect a performance benefit for either one, so choose the vendor of your choice / price point. In my experience, AMD offers a little more performance per euro/dollar, while most of my Hyper-V customers use a standardized Intel setup for all workloads. Just make sure not to mix both vendors in your Hyper-V deployment, and you will be fine.

In terms of memory, you have already learned that a page file does not require any special configuration. Also, the amount of RAM needed by the Hyper-V host is determined and configured automatically, so you can focus on the needs of the virtual machines on the RAM configuration.

Do not use traditional PCI slots on your servers anymore; PCIe offers greatly enhanced performance. Make sure that you use PCIe v3.0 x8 and higher slots for 10-gigabit Ethernet adapters on the server's mainboard to not limit performance at this physical level.

If you have enough adapter slots available on your server system, use multiple NICs with fewer slots instead of single NICs with many ports for optimal performance and redundancy.

Network-hardware-tuning options

Choosing the right network hardware for your Hyper-V hosts can boost up your overall VM performance. There are several hardware features available for supporting the Hyper-V host. You have already read about SMB Direct with RDMA-capable network cards, but there are many more offload capabilities.

Receive Side Scaling (RSS)

RSS is an NIC-driver technology that enables the efficient distribution of network receive processing across multiple CPUs in multiprocessor systems. This basically means that whenever you are *not* using RSS, all the CPU requests to control Hyper-V networking are delivered to the first CPU core. Even if you have four physical CPUs with 12 cores each and with hyper-threading enabled, only the very first core receives these requests. If you use network bandwidths faster than 4 Gb/s, there is a high possibility that you will receive a performance hit when not using RSS. So, make sure that it's available on your NIC, your NIC-driver and activated. If this is the case, these network requests (interrupts) will be spread among all the available CPU cores.

This is the easy part of the story. RSS is only available on the physical host, but not inside virtual machines. Windows Server 2012 R2 offers a solution for this called **Dynamic Virtual Machine Queue (D-VMQ)**. With D-VMQ enabled on our hosts, we can use RSS on our virtual machines.

To see if your adapters are ready for D-VMQ, check via PowerShell:

```
Get-NetAdapterVmq –Name NICName
```

Enable vRSS in one VM via PowerShell:

```
Enable-NetAdapterRSS –Name NICName
```

This was the not-so-easy part of the story. Here comes the hard part: when using vRSS, it blocks some other networking capabilities such as SR-IOV, so you have to choose which one is the best for you. vRSS does not work on virtual NICs (vNICs) attached to the virtual switch on the host management partition like we saw earlier. To use vRSS in your VMs, it's necessary to use D-VMQ at the host level. When using D-VMQ at the host level, you cannot use RSS for your physical NICs on your host OS.

This is why I recommended that you use RDMA-capable network cards for SMB Direct, utilizing live migration to avoid this limitation. We will activate D-VMQ on our physical team that hosts the vSwitch for our virtual machines so that we can leverage vRSS on our VMs. Our host loses RSS capability; however, the heaviest network hits that occur at the host level (live migration and SMB traffic) are handled by SMB Direct with the RDMA network.

The following screenshot shows the Hyper-V guest with vRSS:

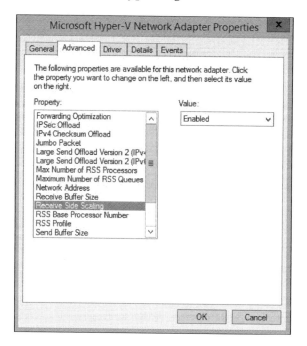

Single Root IO Virtualization

Single Root IO Virtualization (SR-IOV) is another great capability in Hyper-V networking. It allows for a PCIe device, such as an NIC, to be presented to multiple devices, such as virtual machines. Think of it as PCIe virtualization. This only works when it is supported at a physical level (network card), on the server system (BIOS), as well as on **Hyper-V**. SR-IOV offers more performance than VMQ because it uses **Direct Memory Access (DMA)** for direct communication between the physical NIC and the virtual machine. All the other aspects of Hyper-V networking are bypassed so that there is no involvement of NIC Teaming, virtual switches, and other technologies on top of it. This allows for extremely low latency and will be a great option when Hyper-V network virtualization causes CPU impacts through RSS without DMQ, otherwise. However, this also means that if you use NIC Teaming, these NICs cannot be used for SR-IOV, and there is no vSwitch in between that allows for Quality of Service or other management. SR-IOV is compatible with live migration and other Hyper-V features that do not involve network virtualization.

In my experience, SR-IOV is a great choice when handling low-latency, high-bandwidth VMs (for example, VoIP communication) and should be used when the traditional networking model, without SR-IOV, does not deliver enough networking performance. However, it should not be your default option because of the decreased management capabilities.

There is a great blog series about SR-IOV by Microsoft's John Howard available at `http://bit.ly/1uvyagL`. The following screenshot shows communication with and without SR-IOV:

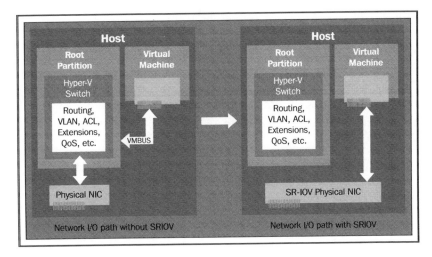

Other offload capabilities

Checksum calculation on your NICs can offload the calculation and validation of the TCP and UDP checksums as well as the IPv4 and IPv6 adapters. This feature should be available and activated on all used network adapters with Hyper-V.

When using network traffic encryption with IPSec, you should use the IPSec offload; otherwise, you will see a 20-30 percent performance hit on your Hyper-V CPUs. However, you should use IPSec only when the security standards of your company tell you to, unless you leave them disabled.

Jumbo frames are another great option to boost network traffic; however, they need end-to-end configuration to work properly. On the physical NICs of the Hyper-V host, configure jumbo frames according to the packet size. The recommendation for most Intel NICs, for example, is an MTU of 9014 bytes. While jumbo frames don't need any configuration on the Hyper-V vSwitch, they need to be configured on the physical switch port as well as on the guest OS NIC. After configuration, you can test your configuration easily using the `ping` command with huge packet sizes:

```
ping -f -l 8500 192.168.1.10
```

It's a best practice to enable jumbo frames if supported by all parts of the chain. It is also compatible with most of the Hyper-V networking features such as RSS, and I highly recommend that you enable it when using ISCSI storage as well.

There are other offloading features, such as **Receive-Segment Coalescing (RSC)**, that reduce the number of IP headers; however, they do not bring any more notable performance benefits to Hyper-V VMs and are therefore not explained further.

For additional details on these features or other advanced Hyper-V network-related performance tunings, visit the network part of *Windows Server Performance Tuning Guidelines* found at `http://bit.ly/1rNpTkR`.

Using IPv6 with Hyper-V

Another common question is about the use of the modern IP protocol, IPv6. It is enabled by default on Windows Server 2012 R2 with Hyper-V, and you better leave it this way. The entire Windows development is done and tested with IPv6 enabled. There can be unforeseen problems occurring after disabling IPv6.

However, if your network standard dictates to disable IPv6, it can be done on the Hyper-V host as well on the VMs. If you decide to disable IPv6, do it only in the registry. We will add the corresponding registry key via PowerShell:

```
New-ItemProperty "HKLM:\SYSTEM\CurrentControlSet\Services\Tcpip6\
Parameters\" -Name "DisabledComponents" -Value 0xffffffff -PropertyType
"DWord"
```

Then, reboot the system. Don't use any other way to disable IPv6, such as unchecking the checkbox in the TCP IP properties of the network card; I've seen problems occurring after that.

I have seen many customers disabling IPv6 via the registry, and some of them had issues with other roles such as Windows Server RRAS. However, I have not seen a single customer experiencing problems with the Hyper-V role with registry-disabled IPv6. So, you are fine until now with this configuration, but it's still not recommended by Microsoft.

Storage-tuning options

In the earlier chapters, you got an overview of the great storage options possible with Hyper-V. Let's now focus on some additional performance tuning for storage. You have seen how dynamically expanding hard disks are a great option for flexibility, especially in combination with thin provisioning, which is supported by Hyper-V on a software-based and hardware-based level. Hyper-V has some special features for the other way around, then data gets deleted. It is important to let the storage subsystem know that the blocks occupied previously are now ready for reuse. If this would not happen, the physical storage system would consider itself full of data, while on a logical level, it would be half empty. In a worst-case situation, you will be unable to write to a non-full drive. Windows Server with Hyper-V uses standardized Trim and Unmap functions. They are enabled by default and don't need any configuration, but you should make sure that your used storage is capable of working with the Trim/Unmap function to maximize storage efficiency. Only Hyper-V-SCSI, an enlightened IDE, and virtual fibre-channel controllers allow the unmap command from the guest to reach the host virtual-storage stack. On the virtual hard disks, only virtual disks formatted as VHDX support unmap commands from the guest. This is another reason to use VHDX files. If you are working with generation 1 VMs, make sure that you use a small IDE-attached system partition and a VHDX file on a SCSI controller for data and applications.

Windows Server with Hyper-V enables a lot of background jobs to consolidate and optimize storage, such as deduplication and defrag jobs. To ensure that these jobs work flawlessly, make sure that you keep at least 10 percent of free space on all drives, including cluster-shared volumes.

Offloaded Data Transfer

Offloaded Data Transfer (ODX) is a great way of speeding up data transfers. If you use an ODX-capable storage, Windows Server with Hyper-V will check before starting a copy job whether there is a faster approach than copying the data on the software stack. It passes a token to the storage subsystem of the copy source and target, and if both tokens are received by an ODX-capable storage system, the copy job will be done at a hardware-assisted level. If the source and target occur on the same system, no data will be copied; just a new link to the same blocks will be created in just a few seconds.

The Hyper-V storage stack also issues ODX operations during maintenance operations for VHDs, such as merging disks after deleting a snapshot:

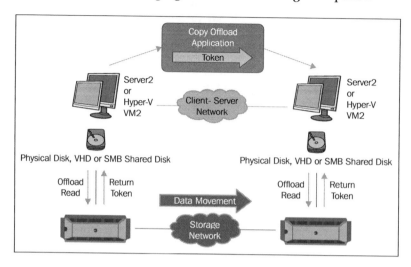

ODX is enabled by default; however, it is again only supported on virtual hard disks that are attached to an SCSI controller. An IDE controller does not support this feature. Also, if your storage subsystem does not support ODX for Windows Server 2012 R2, you should disable it via PowerShell in the registry, as I have seen problems in this combination:

```
Set-ItemProperty HKLM:\SYSTEM\CurrentControlSet\Control\FileSystem -Name
"FilterSupportedFeaturesMode" -Value 1
```

Then, reboot the system after setting the key.

Even if your storage subsystem supports ODX, make sure that you test it before using it in production.

Shutdown-tuning options

There are some additional options to tune the performance of Hyper-V and its VMs; these options are listed in this section.

Setting the shutdown timeout

If you use a Hyper-V cluster and you send a shutdown command to one of its nodes, the node will immediately start a live migration of all the running VMs on this node to free up the node. If you send a shutdown command to a standalone host, it tries to shut down all the VMs. However, it is possible that a cluster node starts rebooting while live migrations and VM shutdown operations are still in progress. This host shutdown time can be configured via the registry. Perform the following steps:

1. Open regedit.
2. Navigate to `HKLM\Cluster\`.
3. Edit the `ShutdownTimeoutInMinutes` value according to your needs.
4. Reboot the system after setting the key.

It might take some experimenting to find out the right value for you; I typically set it no higher than 10 minutes.

Hyper-V benchmarking

After successfully establishing some performance baselines for Hyper-V, it's important to create regular benchmarks of your Hyper-V environment. Use MAP or SCOM to monitor the performance of the common performance counters, but I recommend that you use an overall benchmark from time to time to make sure that the performance on the application level is consistent.

Which type of benchmark you use depends on your workload. I highly recommend a standardized benchmark that utilizes a database and an application tier. The primary benchmark for this is the SAP SD benchmark. If you are a SAP customer, this is the way to go. You can find a Microsoft blog post about a SAP Hyper-V reference benchmark at `http://bit.ly/1nMVSQw`.

If you do not use SAP or another ERP system with this type of benchmark, you can use other available benchmarks. I highly recommend PassMark Performance Test, which is available for a 30-day trial at `http://bit.ly/UFd2Ff`, because it offers benchmarks that utilize all of the hardware resources discussed.

I also recommend SQLIO to test the storage and storage connections available at `http://bit.ly/1obVdIV`.

If you want to use desktop virtualization, you can use the **Login VSI** benchmark; to find out more, check out `http://bit.ly/1pt2roe`.

The results from all these benchmarks are comparable to other Hyper-V setups as well as to other virtualization platforms that do not utilize Hyper-V performance counters.

Hyper-V for virtual desktops

Most of the time, Hyper-V is used to host virtual machines with server operating systems installed. Hyper-V also offers great capabilities to host virtual desktops, but because special licensing is needed, Hyper-V VDI implementations are not seen very often. This topic focuses on using Hyper-V with virtual desktops and its tuning for client operating systems.

Be aware that a VDI deployment is, in most cases, not cheaper than a deployment of remote desktop-session hosts (Terminal Services) but can offer a standardized architecture with a central point of management.

To create a hosting infrastructure for virtual desktops, use the server manager on an existing Windows Server 2012 R2. The **Add Roles** wizard has a full VDI deployment wizard on board. Of course, you can alternatively use PowerShell to install a full VDI environment:

```
New-RDVirtualDesktopDeployment -ConnectionBroker EYVDI01.elanity.de
-WebAccessServer EYVDI02.elanity.de -VirtualizationHost EYVDI03.elanity.de
```

There is also a great end-to-end PowerShell solution available for implementing a VDI scenario in a lab and also for teaching all the necessary PowerShell cmdlets for the VDI setup.

The **Virtual Desktop Infrastructure Starter Kit (VDI SK)** is created by Microsoft's Victor Arzate and is available in the Technet gallery at `http://bit.ly/1pkILFP`. The following screenshot shows the VDI server wizard:

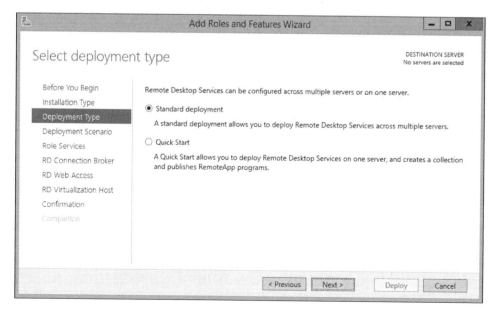

The quick-start setup installs all the VDI-related services on a single operating system instance; this is not recommended in any case. In both cases, a virtual-based desktop deployment is necessary for VDI. Configure the target server for each of the VDI workloads:

- **Remote Desktop Connection Broker**: The RD Connection Broker connects or reconnects a client device to the VDI client (virtual machine)
- **Remote Desktop Web Access**: The RD Web Access Server enables users to connect to its VDI client through session collections and virtual desktop collections, using the web browser
- **Remote Desktop Session Host**: The RD Session Host is a VDI-enabled Hyper-V host

After entering the server names, the further configuration will be done by Server Manager/PowerShell without any need for manual configuration.

If you already have a Hyper-V-ready environment, start by creating a VM template for VDI. Install a new Hyper-V VM with the client operating system of your choice (I highly recommend Windows 8.1 because of its improved VDI features) as the "Golden Image".

After finishing the installation of Windows 8.1, including all the updates and support tools you want to have in every VDI client, run `Sysprep` with the OOBE/generalize option and choose to shut down the system:

```
C:\Windows\System32\Sysprep\Sysprep.exe /OOBe /Generalize /Shutdown /
Mode:VM
```

Using the new `/Mode:VM` switch allows for a faster sysprep, as there is a lot less hardware recognizing for virtual machines necessary as long as you are using the same virtualization environment.

Copy the source VM and specify its path in the next script.

To create a new virtual-desktop collection, use the following PowerShell script:

```
New-RDVirtualDesktopCollection -CollectionName demoPool -PooledManaged
 -VirtualDesktopTemplateName Win81Gold.vhdx
-VirtualDesktopTemplateHostServer EYVDI01
-VirtualDesktopAllocation @{$Servername = 1}
-StorageType LocalStorage
-ConnectionBroker EYVDI02
-VirtualDesktopNamePrefix msVDI
```

> **Licensing hint**
>
> Microsoft uses special licensing around VDI (VDA licenses).
> If you already have your Hyper-V hosts covered by the datacenter
> editions of Windows Server, it can be more economical for you to just
> use single-user-server VMs instead of real client VMs.

Some great performance white papers on VDI are available in project VRC at
`http://bit.ly/1nwr9aK`; they measure the impact of an antivirus or Microsoft
Office in a VDI environment.

Using RemoteFX

Microsoft's **Remote Desktop Protocol (RDP)** is currently available in Version 8.1
and offers great capabilities, including RemoteFX. A little-known fact is that the
RDP 8.1 native client is available for a broad range of platforms, including Windows
7, Windows 8, Windows 8.1, Windows RT, Windows Phone, and also Android and
Apple iOS.

RemoteFX offers some great features around RDP connections, and almost all of
them can be used without special graphic adapters. RemoteFX is enabled by default
and offers features such as multitouch, adaptive graphics, and WAN optimization.
The new RDP client also offers features such as automatic network detection and
RDP over UDP.

RemoteFX is able to detect content by default and load it by priority. Text is loaded
first, then the images are loaded, and at last, the videos and ad banners are loaded
onto the screen. With these capabilities, RDP is not only more performant, but the
performance felt by the user is also significantly improved.

RemoteFX features can be configured via Group Policy as follows:

1. Open the Group Policy Management Console and navigate
   to **ComputerConfiguration | AdministrativeTemplates |
   WindowsComponents | Remote Desktop Services | Remote Desktop
   Session Host | Remote Session Environment**.
2. Edit the **Configure image quality for RemoteFX Adaptive Graphics** setting.
3. Change it from **Default Medium** to **High** or **Lossless** if you want to use
   better graphics. This will consume more bandwidth.
4. Edit the **Configure RemoteFX Adaptive Graphics** setting in the same path.
5. Choose **RemoteFX** to optimize between server scalability or
   bandwidth usage.

6. Edit the **Configure compression for RemoteFX data** setting in the same path.

7. Choose one of **Optimize to use less memory** (but will require more network), **Optimize to use less network bandwidth** (requires more memory), balances memory and network bandwidth and do not use an RDP-compression algorithm. It's highly recommend to use the last option.

8. Edit the **Limit maximum color depth** setting.

9. Select 32 bits per pixel. In my experience, this offers the best performance.

10. Reboot the servers.

 These GPOs must be linked to the virtualization hosts, *not* the virtual desktops or RDSH-VMs that run on top of the virtualization hosts.

There are some other group policies available, but the default settings for them are, most of the time, just fine.

Another way to speed up RDP performance is by adding a powerful GPU to the server. High-end graphic adapters, formerly known only in gaming PCs and CAD workstations, are now available for VDI clients and RDSH VMs. Note that this is currently only supported for generation 1 VMs.

You need to choose a GPO that supports DirectX 11.0 or higher and uses a WDDM 1.2 driver or higher. Make sure that you check the Windows Server Catalog again for RemoteFX GPUs. I have had a good experience with NVIDIA Grid adapters in terms of performance and compatibility. Also, make sure that your Hyper-V host server hardware is capable of running high-end GPUs. The typical server GPU offers only very limited performance and is only using a few of MBs of RAM. RemoteFX GPUs offer great performance and come with gigabytes of graphics RAM. When you want to do more in your VDI VMs or RDSH sessions, then just view the web pages and edit the office files; an RFX GPU might be the right option. It is suitable for running full-HD videos or editing CAD models inside a virtual machine. With Hyper-V on Windows Server 2012 R2, you can even share a GPU between numerous virtual machines.

To add a GPU to a virtual machine, use the following PowerShell cmdlet:

```
Add-VMRemoteFx3dVideoAdapter -VMName EyVM01
```

To specify the resolution you want to use inside the VM, use the following PowerShell cmdlet:

```
SET-VMRemoteFx3dVideoAdapter -VMName EyVM01 -MaximumResolution 1920x1200
```

When using RemoteFX adapters with VDI VMs, it's a best practice to calculate the increased memory usage. A Windows 8.1 VM should then be deployed with the possibility to use up to 4 GB of RAM. In a non-RemoteFX vGPU scenario, 2 GB of RAM is enough in most scenarios. VDI clients with Windows 8.1 work well with dynamic memory and two CPU cores, so this should be the default setup. I often see VDI workloads deployed with differencing disks. This isn't optimal from a performance point of view, and additionally, this is a management nightmare as VMM cannot work with differencing disks. It's a far better option to use dynamic VHDX files and activate the Windows integrated deduplication, which you learned in *Chapter 4, Storage Best Practices*.

Other than that, virtual machines that run a VDI workload are just another bunch of Hyper-V VMs.

Summary

By the end of this chapter, you would have implemented a lot of possible performance optimizations for your Hyper-V environment, and you don't need to fear the production usage of your setup. You would have tightened your server hardware, storage, and network as well as the Hyper-V role configuration for optimal-usage scenarios.

Continue now to *Chapter 7, Management with System Center*, to learn more about managing your Hyper-V hosts, its virtual machines, and the complete fabric, with Microsoft's management suite, **System Center**. You will also learn more about the deployment, monitoring, backup, and automation of Hyper-V.

7
Management with System Center

"Every datacenter and cloud infrastructure needs an efficient management solution. With System Center, Microsoft offers a great solution for managing, automating, and monitoring your datacenter.

Especially, Virtual Machine Manager allows you to integrate your hardware resources – such as storage, networking, and compute – and manage them from a single pane of glass."

Thomas Maurer - MVP Hyper-V

Your Hyper-V environment is now configured for high performance, and you are probably expanding the use of Hyper-V by now. This chapter gives you an overview of the management of Hyper-V servers through various system center components.

In this chapter, we will cover the following topics:

- Deployment and management with System Center Virtual Machine Manager for:
    - Service templates
    - Fabric management

- Monitoring with System Center Operations Manager
- Backup with System Center Data Protection Manager
- Automation with System Center

Microsoft System Center

Microsoft System Center 2012 R2 is Microsoft's solution for advanced managing of Windows Server and its components, along with its dependencies such as various hardware and software products. It consists of various components that support every stage of your IT services from planning to operating over backup to automation. System Center has existed since 1994 and has evolved continuously. It now offers a great set of tools for very efficient management of server and client infrastructures. It also offers the ability to create and operate whole clouds—run in your own data center or a public cloud data center such as Microsoft Azure. Today, it's your choice whether to run your workloads on-premises or off-premises. System Center provides a standardized set of tools for a unique and consistent Cloud OS management experience.

System Center does not add any new features to Hyper-V, but it does offer great ways to make the most out of it and ensure streamlined operating processes after its implementation. System Center is licensed via the same model as Windows Server is, leveraging Standard and Datacenter Editions on a physical host level. While every System Center component offers great value in itself, the binding of multiple components into a single workflow offers even more advantages:

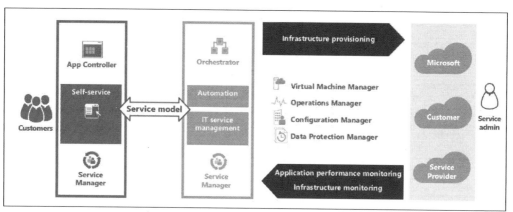

System Center overview

When do you need System Center? There is no right or wrong answer to this and the most given answer by any IT consultant around the world is "It depends."

System Center adds value to any IT environment starting with only a few systems. In my experience, a Hyper-V environment with up to three hosts and 15 VMs can be managed efficiently without the use of System Center. If you plan to use more hosts or virtual machines, System Center will definitely be a great solution for you. Let's take a look at the components of System Center.

System Center Virtual Machine Manager

System Center Virtual Machine Manager (SCVMM) is not another hypervisor besides Hyper-V. VMM simply adds a management functionality to virtualization hosts. It works best with Hyper-V but is also capable of managing day-to-day operational tasks for VMware vSphere through vCenter and Citrix XenServer hosts.

You can create your own virtual machine templates with VMM for fast deployment of new virtual machines with a basic set of content and configuration. VMM takes the approach of predefined templates to a new level, by service templates. A service template not only consists of a virtual machine and a preinstalled operating system but also offers much more, starting from the integration of software components such as databases and applications over storage to load-balanced network connections. All you need to do is define a central service template that offers dynamic expanding or shrinking of the VM environment, purely based on current performance requirements. Applications consisting of database servers, application servers, and frontend servers are ideal candidates for service templates. There are several service templates available for download at **TechNet Gallery** (`http://bit.ly/VYK8jh`), one is shown in the following screenshot:

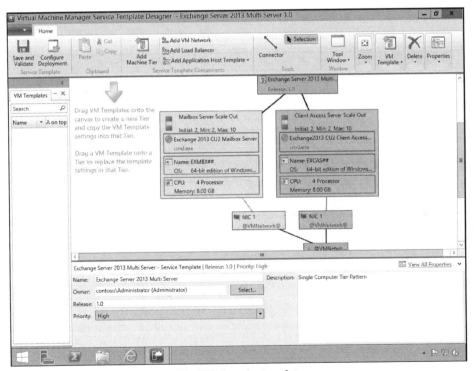

The VMM service template

After installing SCVMM, follow these steps for its basic configuration:

1. Add your Hyper-V hosts to SCVMM by adding SCVMM agents to the corresponding Hyper-V hosts. This enables the management of your Hyper-V hosts and VMs through SCVMM. The SCVMM installation and agent installation is described at `http://bit.ly/1wXMBLR`.

2. Create host groups and clouds to allow for delegated and granular management. You can use host groups to group virtual machine hosts in meaningful ways, often based on a physical site location and resource allocation. This configuration is described at `http://bit.ly/1vZ3O3j`.

3. Configure the VMM library. The VMM library is a catalog of resources that provides access to file-based resources such as virtual hard disks, ISO images, and scripts, as well as virtual machines, service templates, and profiles that reside in the VMM database. This configuration is described at `http://bit.ly/1uhyrzD`.

4. Configure VMM network management. Networking in VMM includes multiple enhancements that enable you — the administrator — to efficiently provision network resources for a virtualized environment. This configuration is described at `http://bit.ly/1owqj9W`.

5. Configure VMM storage management. To connect VMM with your storage fabric, follow this guide at `http://bit.ly/1u416cv`.

Cloud management

Can we include storage in a VMM service template? Yes, because the **virtual machine manager (VMM)** offers a full fabric management solution on various levels:

- For servers, the following solution is available:

    ○ VMM can create a connection to the BMC controller of a physical server system. VMM is capable of booting the server system, configuring it based on your needs, and performing a bare metal installation of a Hyper-V host, complete clusters, or Windows file servers.

- For storage, the following solutions are available:

    ○ Connect to your storage infrastructure, that is, a SAN, a scale out file server, or an iSCSI target, and manage it via VMM. It is possible to create deployment workflows, where VMM automatically expands storage volumes or creates a new one. It is also capable of mounting or unmounting storage nodes to a new cluster node.

- Use storage pooling on gold, silver, or bronze to differentiate between low-performance storage such as your test server, iSCSI target, and an enterprise SAN from your VMM management console. You need to provide the correct storage for use with appropriate access. VMM is a fully trained storage administrator.

- For a network, the following solutions are available:

    - VMM offers great value for network management. Via VMM, you can manage Hyper-V network virtualization on a logical network level, completely independent of the physical network setup. Create VM networks and provide automatically assigned static IP addresses to your virtual machines via **IP Address Management (IPAM)**.

    - Create a load balancer on a software level (Windows NLB) or manage the existing the hardware load balancer such as F5.

VMM offers a lot more than fabric management:

- Create your own clouds for delegated access to a service consisting of different virtual machines and fabric components

- Delegate administration for a cloud to allow their owners to create new VM resources based on predefined quotas

- Select a prepared virtual machine and service template bound to specific clouds and users can spin up new VMs and whole groups of VMs in just a few minutes without the need to involve any IT personnel

- Use chargeback or showback reports to identify the amount of used resources and their costs

Another great feature of VMM is the optionally enabled function to dynamically move virtual machines between your cluster nodes to distribute the load. You can also go the other way around and consolidate virtual machines on fewer hosts and power off the unneeded cluster nodes, until the performance is needed again and the host is powered on again. All this is handled automatically by VMM without manual intervention.

To learn more about VMM, refer to *System Center 2012 R2 Virtual Machine Manager Cookbook, Edvaldo Alessandro Cardoso, Packt Publishing,* at http://bit.ly/1vBjf4i.

System Center App Controller

System Center App Controller (SCAC) provides a self-service portal to VMM. It allows the management and deployment of virtual machines from a web-based console without the need for additional client consoles. It uses the VMM database to access content and quota management. My favorite feature of an SCAC is the possibility to manage not only your on-premise VMs, but also virtual machines hosted in a public cloud such as Microsoft Azure in one or multiple Azure subscriptions. SCAC even offers the functionality to move virtual machines between both worlds. It is also possible to deploy your on-premise-generated virtual machine templates to the cloud through an SCAC.

After installing SCAC, there are two main tasks:

- Add your SCVMM clouds to an SCAC. The installation of an SCAC and the integration of VMM is described at `http://bit.ly/Y47OVg`.

- Add your Microsoft Azure subscriptions to SCAC. This step is described at `http://bit.ly/Y47OVg`.

To learn more on SCAC, visit this free e-book at `http://bit.ly/1m2D6R5`.

System Center Operations Manager

System Center Operations Manager (SCOM) is an end-to-end monitoring tool offering a great transparency to your infrastructure. While many monitoring solutions are available in the market, there are none as sophisticated as SCOM. While other solutions monitor a given set of up to 30 parameters per host, such as checking for free space on drives, pinging systems, and checking whether a specific Windows service is running, SCOM offers far more value.

With hundreds and thousands of preconfigured rulesets monitoring your environment, delivered in management packs, OM not only detects the exact location and source of the problem but also delivers great guidance on how to work around an incident or apply a permanent solution without the need to leave the SCOM console.

These management packs are free for download for all Microsoft products and ready to use. You don't need to put more time into configuration than into other monitoring solutions that do not offer this granularity. This great concept of an SCOM allows you to avoid many problems before there is an impact on production systems, such as receiving notifications via an instant messenger or e-mail, or create automatic recovery tasks in the event of an error.

You can receive all relevant performance information about your systems, including Hyper-V hosts and VMs. You can also monitor the network devices and switches connected to your Hyper-V environment as well as the application-level performance of web applications such as the self-service portal. With SCOM, you can forward the collected information to your trouble-stricken system, that is, System Center Service Manager, and close the ticket when the problem gets resolved. With this great level of detail, SCOM is even capable of calculating future performance requirements based on your usage in the past.

For advanced scenarios, Microsoft's partner, Veeam offers a commercial Hyper-V management pack allowing you to go even further into the Hyper-V stack from a monitoring perspective. The SCOM screen looks as follows:

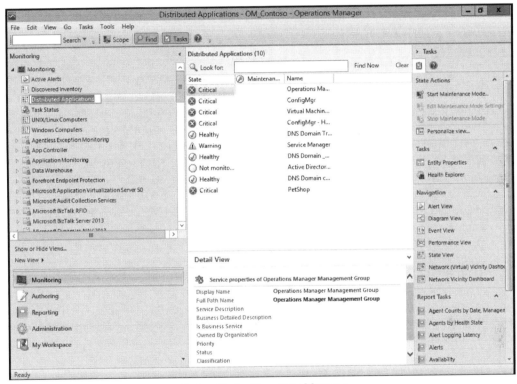

System Center Operations Manager

Here are the main steps to get SCOM up and running:

1. Install your SCOM servers. You will typically install two SCOM servers: one as your primary monitoring server and the other as data warehouse. The installation and basic configuration is described at `http://bit.ly/1r0by4u`.

2. Add SCOM agents to your Hyper-V hosts and VMs through the SCOM **Discovery Wizard** to enable monitoring. This configuration is described at `http://bit.ly/1uhBvMj`.

3. Import the necessary Hyper-V management packs. This process is described at `http://bit.ly/VZitid`.

For additional information on SCOM, visit this virtual academy course at `http://bit.ly/1wXQkZS`.

System Center Service Manager

Microsoft's **Service Manager (SM)** is often described as the Microsoft version of a helpdesk tool. However, SCSM offers a lot more than that and is a fully capable IT service management tool. With SCSM, you can document incidents and problems, plan the next software release, and start document planned changes. An SCSM is the most central component where all the data comes together. Through integrated connectors, the collected data from all other System Center components are centralized in a complete **Configuration Management Database (CMDB)** and allows you to pull more value out of this data. Its SharePoint-based self-service portal allows for end user communication and web-based creation of incidents and service requests. An SCSM comes with a set of built-in best practice processes for core ITIL components. ITIL and MOF are a set of best practice descriptions on IT service management processes.

By orchestrating this knowledge across the various System Center components, an SCSM helps IT staff to continuously adapt to new requirements while lowering costs and reducing time to resolution. This is the reason why an SCSM is a great tool for aligning your IT to your business needs. You can use Service-Level Agreements to proof this value with SCSM functionalities.

You can also leverage the great data resource pool to create transparent reporting for optimization, or use a chargeback- /showback-based reporting for virtual machine resources.

The following screenshot shows the SCSM screen:

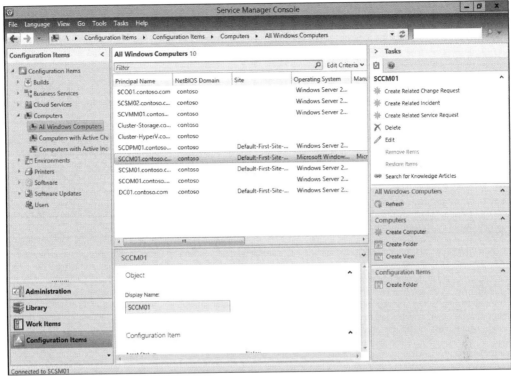

System Center Service Manager

You can use SLA dashboards with SCSM to demonstrate the great performance of IT on the company's Intranet portal, or use huge Excel spreadsheets for optimization.

SCSM offers even further value through various partner extensions from companies such as Cireson, Opslogix, or Provance, including full asset management solutions.

The main steps to get your SCSM (installation described here: `http://bit.ly/1qhhQg6`) up and running are as follows:

1. Register your data warehouse server after its installation. This is described at `http://bit.ly/1pxWgEK`.
2. Deploy the self-service portal to enable end user interaction. This is described at `http://bit.ly/1Ch1wAT`.
3. Configure SCSM connectors to import data from the various System Center components to create a complete CMDB solution. This is described at `http://bit.ly/1Ch1Dwn`.

For additional information on SCSM, visit this book, `http://bit.ly/1owrQwD`.

System Center Orchestrator

Many existing solutions come with integrated workflow solutions. Think of Microsoft Exchange Server automatically sending an *out of office* notification or of Microsoft SQL Server executing maintenance plans. All these workflow solutions are contained in the product they are part of.

System Center Orchestrator (SCOR) is a great addition to Hyper-V and SCSM. Orchestrator provides a workflow management solution for the data center. Orchestrator lets you automate the creation, monitoring, and deployment of resources in your environment through workflows known as runbooks. With System SCOR, it is, for instance, possible to span runbooks originating from SCSM to Hyper-V involving, for instance, Microsoft Azure, Microsoft Exchange, and Oracle databases. This greatly simplifies performing daily operations because now you can automate every reoccurring technical process. Starting with user creation in different systems over VM deployment with automatic backup and restore, up to a fully scripted disaster recovery failover solution—SCOR is capable of building and executing these workflows:

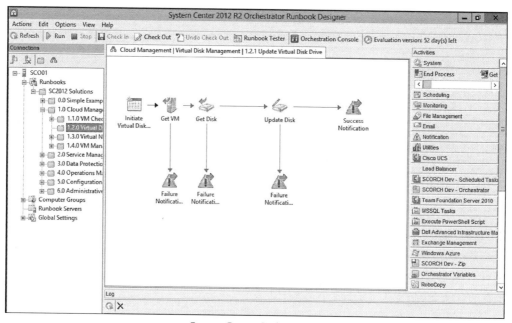

System Center Orchestrator

Many best practice runbooks around Hyper-V are already built, involving great solutions for automated Hyper-V Replica failover or the creation of virtual machines on Hyper-V with several dependencies. If you have done anything twice in IT, SCOR is the right component to use.

The main steps to get your SCOR installation (described here: `http://bit.ly/1nh9yQv`) up and running:

1. Download integration packs and add-ons. This is necessary to connect your runbooks to your infrastructure. This configuration is described at `http://bit.ly/1nh9Sia`.

2. Design your first orchestrator runbook as described in this free e-book: `http://bit.ly/1Ch2ld3`.

For additional information on orchestrator, you can refer to *Microsoft System Center 2012 Orchestrator Cookbook, Samuel Erskine (MCT), Packt Publishing*, at `http://bit.ly/1B8tMUY`.

System Center Data Protection Manager

Microsoft's DPM is the bigger version of Windows Server backup (wbadmin) and itself a complete backup and recovery solution. You can back up Hyper-V clusters on the host level without the need to install backup agents into every virtual machine. You can take consistent backups of running Hyper-V VMs or powered-off virtual machines replicated through Hyper-V Replica. To support the backup of deduplicated volumes, SCDPM is a great backup tool for saving space. SCDPM is also capable of protecting Hyper-V VMs by backing up the replica and not the primary VM. For host-level backups, a SCDPM agent is installed on the Hyper-V host and will protect the entire VM running on that Hyper-V host. For guest-level backup, a SCDPM agent is installed within the VM operating system and is used to protect the workload present within that VM.

SCDPM does not create backups on a classic multirotation principle with frequently occurring full backups. SCDPM uses a more modern approach, creating a single full backup only, followed by incremental forever backups every 15 minutes. This removes the classic load-heavy backup window in the middle of the night leading to hours of data loss in a restore. Having recovery points every 15 minutes available offers great point-in-time recovery options, while it's only backing up changed blocks, without the need to rebackup and save the same data over and over again.

It is possible to replicate created backups to another SCDPM server, to a tape device, or to Microsoft Azure. This replaces the need for manual tape rotation and secured offsite transport. The data is scored and transmitted with full encryption.

SCDPM can back up and restore all typical Microsoft workloads in the physical and virtual world, such as Windows Server with Hyper-V:

- Exchange Server
- SQL Server
- SharePoint Server
- Microsoft Dynamics

Remember that Linux VMs running on Hyper-V are also supported Microsoft workloads. In fact, it's easier to run a consistent backup of a Linux system running on Hyper-V than on a physical level. Microsoft has included a **Volume Shadow Copy Service (VSS)** for the Linux driver in the Hyper-V integration components for leveraging this capability. SCDPM can protect your Hyper-V environment using SMB shares as well, but this requires installation of the SCDPM agent on all servers using the SMB remote storage.

SCDPM is supported to perform an **item level recovery (ILR)** of a VM, even if the SCDPM server itself is running as a VM. SCDPM is able to perform an ILR by indexing the VHDs/VHDXs associated with the VM. The SCDPM is shown here:

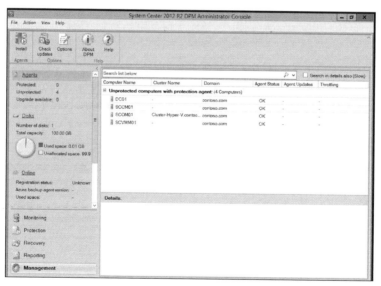

System Center Data Protection Manager

After the installation of SCDPM (described here: `http://bit.ly/1sTugJj`), follow these steps for a basic configuration:

1. Add SCDPM storage for saving backups. This essential step is described here: `http://bit.ly/1tmBhX7`.

2. Install SCDPM protection agents to your Hyper-V hosts and VMs. These agents will communicate to your SCDPM server. The configuration is described here: `http://bit.ly/VZkWcu`.

3. Create a Protection Group to configure your backup job. This configuration is described here: `http://bit.ly/VZljDK`.

For additional information on SCDPM, you can refer to this book: `http://bit.ly/1rHWKKd`.

There are other System Center components available such as Configuration Manager and Endpoint Protection; however, these tools are mostly client-focused and will not be covered in this book; however, they can be utilized for server management as well. Keep in mind that System Center is available for a 180-day trial period, so try it out today.

Automatic System Center deployment

Installing System Center with its various components is a complex and time-consuming task. Microsoft's Rob Willis created the **PowerShell Deployment Toolkit (PDT)**, which allows the unattended installation of all System Center components in under 2 hours instead of spending days manually installing everything. The following are the features of PDT:

- PDT downloads all prerequirements for System Center
- Automatically creates the virtual machines necessary, hosting the System Center installations including operating systems
- Creates the corresponding Active Directory Domain and service accounts
- Installs all System Center prerequirements
- Installs all System Center components of your choice
- Configures basic integration between the installed System Center components

PDT is a great way to create a lab environment quickly for evaluation, but even production setups can be installed through PDT. PDT utilizes XML files for configuration. The required customization of these XML files can be a tricky job. To simplify this process, I have created the PDT GUI together with my coworker, Kamil Kosek.

PDT GUI offers a user interface to edit the XML files necessary for PDT and adds some management improvements for the various PDT components.

PDT and PDT GUI can be downloaded from `http://aka.ms/PDTGUI` and are available for free. The following screenshot shows PDT with PDT GUI:

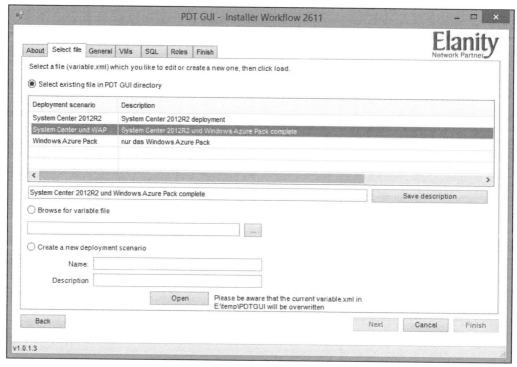

PDT with PDT GUI

Summary

After finishing this chapter, you now have an overview of the great capabilities added on top of Hyper-V when running System Center. You can use automatic deployment and operating processes while maintaining great data security through improved backups.

In *Chapter 8, Migration to Hyper-V 2012 R2*, we will learn how to move the existing workloads from physical systems and other hypervisors to Microsoft's virtualization solution Hyper-V.

A more detailed overview on System Center is available in a free e-book; you can download it from `http://bit.ly/1pZQHyj`.

8
Migration to Hyper-V 2012 R2

"With the experience of doing several hundred migrations, I have collected some good best practices: do some thorough investigation before moving regarding what is running on those migration objects and preferably do some performance analysis also. After migration from another vendor, do some cleaning of third party software such as VMware tools or raid tools and install the latest VM additions, which can be done automatically."

Niklas Akerlund MVP – Hyper-V

By now, you should be aware of all the important best practices of Hyper-V. To take advantage of all these benefits, it's highly recommended to use the latest version of Hyper-V—2012 R2. If you are running any older versions of Hyper-V, it is now time to move on. In this chapter, you will learn about the various tools and methods used for upgrading Hyper-V to 2012 R2.

The following topics will be covered in this chapter:

- Export/import/recreation of VMs
- Cross-version Live Migration
- Copy Cluster Roles Wizard
- **Microsoft Virtual Machine Converter (MVMC)** and **Microsoft Automation Toolkit (MAT)**
- Project Shift for MAT and other third-party solutions
- **Physical to Virtual (P2V)** conversions
- Virtualized domain controllers

Upgrading single Hyper-V hosts

If you are currently running a single host with an older version of Hyper-V and now want to upgrade this host on the same hardware, there is a limited set of decisions to be made. You want to upgrade the host with the least amount of downtime and without losing any data from your virtual machine. Before you start the upgrade process, make sure all components from your infrastructure are compatible with the new version of Hyper-V. Then it's time to prepare your hardware for this new version of Hyper-V by upgrading all firmware to the latest available version and downloading the necessary drivers for Windows Server 2012 R2 with Hyper-V along with its installation media.

One of the most crucial questions in this update scenario is whether you should use the integrated installation option called **in-place upgrade**, where the existing operating system will be transformed to the recent version of Hyper-V or delete the current operating system and perform a clean installation.

While the installation experience of in-place upgrades works well when only the Hyper-V role is installed, based on experiences, some versions of upgraded systems are more likely to suffer problems. Numbers pulled from the Elanity support database show about 15 percent more support cases on upgraded systems from Windows Server 2008 R2 than clean installations. Remember how fast and easy it is nowadays to do a clean install of Hyper-V; this is why it is highly recommended to do this over upgrading existing installations. If you are currently using Windows Server 2012 and want to upgrade to Windows Server 2012 R2, we have not yet seen any differences in the number of support cases between the installation methods. However, being so fast and easy with clean installations of Hyper-V, I barely use them.

Before starting any type of upgrade scenario, make sure you have current backups of all affected virtual machines.

Nonetheless, if you want to use the in-place upgrade, insert the Windows Server 2012 R2 installation media and run this command from your current operating system:

```
Setup.exe /auto:upgrade
```

If it fails, it's most likely due to an incompatible application installed on the older operating system. Start the setup without the parameter to find out which applications need to be removed before executing the unattended setup.

If you upgrade from Windows Server 2012, there is no additional preparation needed; if you upgrade from older operating systems, make sure to remove all snapshots from your virtual machines.

Importing virtual machines

If you choose to do a clean installation of the operating systems, you do not necessarily have to export the virtual machines first; just make sure all VMs are powered off and are stored on a different partition than your Hyper-V host OS. If you are using a SAN, disconnect all LUNs before the installation and reconnect them afterwards to ensure their integrity through the installation process. To install the new operating system on the host, just follow the procedures showed in *Chapter 1, Accelerate Hyper-V Deployment*. After completion of the procedure, just reconnect the LUNs and set the disk online in diskpart or **Control Panel | Computer Management | Disk Management**.

If you are using local disks, make sure not to reformat the partition with your virtual machines on it. Set the partition online and then reimport the virtual machines. Before you start the reimport process, make sure all dependencies of your virtual machines are available, especially vSwitches.

To import a single Hyper-V VM, use the following PowerShell cmdlet:

```
IMPORT-VM -Path 'D:\VMs\EyVM01\Virtual Machines\2D5EECDA-8ECC-4FFC-ACEE-
66DAB72C8754.xml'
```

To import all virtual machines from a specific folder, use this command:

```
Get-ChildItem d:\VMs -Recurse -Filter "Virtual Machines" | %{Get-
ChildItem $_.FullName -Filter *.xml} | %{import-vm $_.FullName -Register}
```

After that, all VMs are registered and ready for use on your new Hyper-V hosts. Make sure to update the Hyper-V integration services of all virtual machines before going back into production. If you still have virtual disks in the old .vhd format, it's now time to convert them to .vhdx files. Use this PowerShell cmdlet on powered-off VMs or standalone vDisk to convert a single .vhd file:

```
Convert-VHD -Path d:\VMs\testvhd.vhd -DestinationPath d:\VMs\testvhdx.
vhdx
```

If you want to convert the disks of all your VMs, fellow MVPs, Aidan Finn and Didier van Hoye, provided a great end-to-end solution to achieve this. This can be found here: http://bit.ly/1omOagi.

I often hear from customers they don't want to upgrade their disks, so as to be able to revert to older versions of Hyper-V when needed. First, you should know that I have never met a customer who has done that, because there really is no technical reason why anyone should do this. Second, even if you would do this backwards move, it is not supported to run virtual machines on older Hyper-V hosts, if they had been deployed on more modern versions of Hyper-V before. The reason for this is very simple; Hyper-V does not offer a way for downgrading Hyper-V integration services. The only way to move a virtual machine back to an older Hyper-V host is by restoring a backup of the VM made earlier before the upgrade process.

Exporting virtual machines

If you want to use another physical system running a newer version of Hyper-V, you have multiple possible options:

- When using a SAN as a shared storage, make sure all your virtual machines, including their virtual disks, are located on other LUNs rather than on the host operating system. Disconnect all LUNs hosting virtual machines from the source host and connect them to the target host. Bulk import the VMs from the specified folders.

- When using SMB3 shared storage from scale-out file servers, make sure to switch access to the shares hosting VMs to the new Hyper-V hosts.

- When using local hard drives and upgrading from Windows Server 2008 SP2 or Windows Server 2008 R2 with Hyper-V, it's necessary to export the virtual machines to a storage location reachable from the new host. Hyper-V servers running legacy versions of the OS (prior to 2012 R2) need to power off the VMs before an export can occur. To export a virtual machine from a host, use the following PowerShell cmdlet:

    ```
    Export-VM -Name EyVM -Path D:\
    ```

- To export all virtual machines to a folder underneath the following root, use the following command:

    ```
    Get-VM | Export-VM -Path D:\
    ```

- In most cases, it is also possible to just copy the virtual machine folders containing virtual hard disk's and configuration files to the target location and import them to Windows Server 2012 R2 Hyper-V hosts. However, the export method is more reliable and should be preferred.

- A good alternative for moving virtual machines can be the re-creation of virtual machines. If you have another host up and running with a recent version of Hyper-V, it may be a good opportunity to also upgrade some guest OSes. For instance, Windows Server 2003 and 2003 R2 are running out of extended support by July 2015. Depending on your applications, it may now be the right choice to create new virtual machines with Windows Server 2012 R2 as a guest operating system and migrate your existing workloads from older VMs to these new machines.

- When using Windows Server 2012 and local hard drives, take a look at the cross-version Live Migration feature explained next in this chapter.

Cross-version Live Migration

One of the great improvements in Windows Server 2012 R2 is the ability to move the running virtual machines between hosts that run a different version of Hyper-V in a defined environment. Cross-version Live Migration simplifies the migration process from Windows Server 2012 to Windows Server 2012 R2 for Hyper-V hosts. The same way you can use the **Shared-Nothing Live Migration** to move a VM and its storage to another standalone Hyper-V host. While the VM is running, you can now execute a Shared-Nothing Live Migration cross-version. This only works from Windows Server 2012 to its successor Windows Server 2012 R2 and not in any other combination. It also works on clusters. While moving all the storage of the VMs takes a long time, this is the recommended migration option if you want to reduce downtime—there is none, at least at the migration process—you still need to reboot the virtual machines after upgrading the integration services of the guest VMs.

If you are using SMB3 Fileshares as storage for your virtual machines, you don't even need to transfer the virtual disks with it, and a cross-version Live Migration does not take longer than a Live Migration between the cluster nodes.

Make sure that the source and destination Hyper-V hosts are in the same Active Directory domain or in a trusted domain. This can even be hosted in a different forest. In the case of remote domains, make sure the name resolution is working both ways. Configure vSwitches on the destination hosts to map the source hosts' networks, only then can a successful Live Migration occur.

Cross-version Live Migration works the same way as a Shared-Nothing Live Migration you already learned about. You can trigger it via PowerShell, Hyper-V Manager, Failover Cluster Manager, or System Center Virtual Machine Manager.

The Copy Cluster Roles Wizard

After learning how to upgrade single Hyper-V hosts, let's now take a look at a nice little tool to speed things up when using clustered Hyper-V instances. On Windows Server 2012 and Windows Server 2012 R2, the Copy Cluster Roles Wizard, formally known as Cluster Migration Wizard, is available.

With the Copy Cluster Roles Wizard, it is possible to move the roles of whole Hyper-V clusters to another Hyper-V cluster, including a cross-version migration of all virtual machines. The Copy Cluster Roles Wizard does not initiate cross-version Live Migrations, it requires a manual storage unmap.

The Copy Cluster Roles Wizard is primarily used in conjunction with SAN volumes. It connects to the source cluster, copies all vital cluster information such as role configuration, and allows to just map the storage LUNs from your SAN to your new cluster and start all cluster roles back in a matter of a few seconds. This process is very fast and comfortable; however, it requires a simultaneous downtime for all hosted virtual machines.

You can start the Copy Cluster Roles Wizard from the cluster properties at **Failover Cluster Manager**. I have not seen a PowerShell equivalent yet.

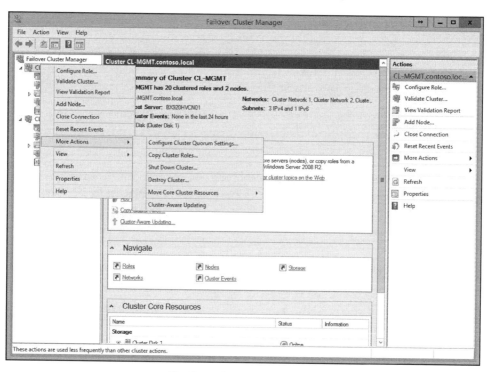

The Copy Cluster Roles Wizard

The first information you need to provide to the Copy Cluster Roles Wizard is the name of the old source cluster. The wizard connects to the old cluster and reads in its cluster and role configurations. You will see a list of cluster roles found on the old cluster and ready for migration. Be aware that you can only migrate complete cluster shared volumes with all virtual machines hosted on it. If you are using a traditional one VM per LUN model, you can select individual VMs for migration.

You even have the option to migrate the cluster core roles with its cluster DNS name and IP address. However, this complicates the migration process and is not recommended. Choose unique cluster names and IP addresses for a smooth process.

If you are still using pass-through disks on your virtual machines, disconnect them before the migration process and convert them afterwards to VHDX files. There are some issues with pass-through disk migrations that can be avoided this way.

In my example, I'm using the Failover Cluster Manager connected to a Hyper-V cluster running Windows Server 2012 R2, **CL-MGMT.contoso.com**. I want to move two test resources from the **CL-Prod.contoso.com** cluster running Windows Server 2012:

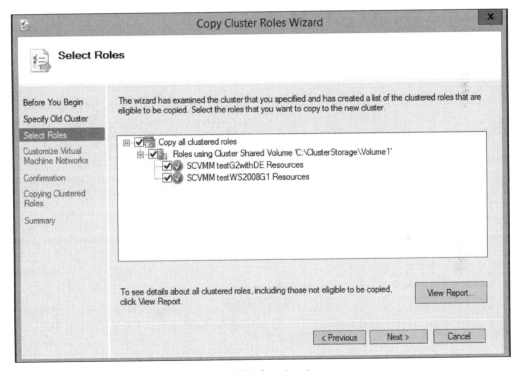

Select VMs for migration

On the next screen, map the networks used by the virtual machines by selecting the corresponding virtual switches:

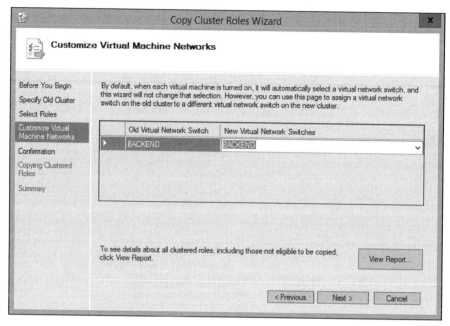

Network mapping

After that, you will receive a report of what exactly will happen during the copying role process. This all can still occur while the source cluster is online and its VMs are up and running. When continuing to the next step in the wizard, the selected cluster roles will be copied to the target cluster. They will be absolutely identical in terms of technical IDs, names, and configurations. Their state is different, while still running on the source cluster, they are powered off on the target cluster.

The new cluster is now prestaged as far as possible, this is as far as it goes without downtime, the wizard is completed. The remaining steps need to be done manually:

1. You now need to shut down all VMs on the source cluster so that its cluster resources reaches the offline state.

2. Open the SAN administration console of your storage systems and unmask the LUNs presented to the source Hyper-V hosts. Map them to your target Hyper-V hosts. Make really sure the LUNs are *never* presented to both the clusters simultaneously, this could destroy all your data!

3. Refresh the cluster console and import the new storage volumes.

4. Start all virtual machines on the target cluster.

All your virtual machines should be up and running in only a few minutes. Make sure to check all VMs for their dependent resources, that is, whether every Network Interface Card is mapped correctly to its corresponding virtual switch. Check the host's event log for any problems.

After you have ensured that all your services are running, shut down the source cluster and reinstall it with the current operating system, in order to add them to your new cluster if compatible.

Migrating VMware virtual machines

If you are running virtual machines on VMware ESXi hosts, there are really good options available for moving them to Hyper-V. There are different approaches on how to convert a VMware virtual machine to Hyper-V: from the inside of the VM on a guest level, on host level, running cold conversions with the VM powered off, running hot conversions on a running VM, and so on. I will give you a short overview of the currently available tools in the market.

System Center VMM

You have already seen the System Center VMM in earlier chapters for fabric and cloud management. SCVMM can also be used for a limited set of **Virtual to Virtual (V2V)** conversions of its VMs. SCVMM V2V functions don't have any recent updates and are prone to errors. SCVMM should not be the first tool of your choice, take a look at MVMC combined with MAT to get an equal functionality from a better working tool.

The earlier versions of SCVMM allowed for online or offline conversions of VMs, the current version, 2012 R2, allows only for offline conversions of VMs. Select a powered-off VM on a VMware host or from the SCVMM library share to start the conversion. The VM conversion will convert VMware-hosted virtual machines through vCenter and ensure that the entire configuration, such as memory, virtual processor, and other machine configurations, are also migrated from the initial source. The tool also adds virtual NICs to the deployed virtual machine on Hyper-V.

The VMware tools must be uninstalled before the conversion, because you won't be able to remove the VMware tools when the VM is not running on a VMware host. SCVMM 2012 R2 supports ESXi hosts running 4.1 and 5.1 but not the latest ESX Version 5.5. SCVMM conversions are great to automate through their integrated PowerShell support and it's very easy to install upgraded Hyper-V integration services as part of setup or adding any kind of automation through PowerShell or System Center Orchestrator. Besides manually removing VMware tools, using SCVMM is an end-to-end solution in the migration process. You can find some PowerShell examples for SCVMM-powered V2V conversion scripts here: `http://bit.ly/Y4bGp8`.

Microsoft Virtual Machine Converter

Microsoft released its first version of the free solution accelerator **Microsoft Virtual Machine Converter** (**MVMC**) in 2013 and should be available in Version 3.0 by the release of this book. MVMC provides a small and easy option to migrate selected virtual machines to Hyper-V. MVMC takes a very similar approach to the conversion as SCVMM does. The conversion happens at a host level and offers a fully integrated end-to-end solution. MVMC supports all recent versions of VMware vSphere. MVMC will even uninstall the VMware tools and install the Hyper-V integration services. MVMC 2.0 works with all supported Hyper-V guest operating systems, including Linux.

MVMC comes with a full GUI wizard as well as a fully scriptable **command-line interface** (**CLI**). Besides being a free tool, it is fully supported by Microsoft in case you experience any problems during the migration process. MVMC should be the first tool of your choice if you do not know which tool to use. Like most other conversion tools, MVMC does the actual conversion on the MVMC server itself and requires its disk space to host the original VMware virtual disk as well as the converted Hyper-V disk. MVMC even offers an add-on for VMware virtual center servers to start conversions directly from the vSphere console.

The current release of MVMC is freely available at its official download site: `http://bit.ly/1kzs2Aa`.

Download MVMC to the conversion system and start the click-through setup. After finishing the download, start the MVMC with the GUI by executing `Mvmc.Gui.exe`. The wizard guides you through some choices:

1. MVMC is not only capable of migrating to Hyper-V, but also allows you to move virtual machines to Microsoft Azure.

2. Select Hyper-V as a target.

3. Enter the name of the Hyper-V host you want this VM to run on and specify a Fileshare to use and the format of the disks you want to create. Choosing the **Dynamically expanding** disks should be the best option most of the time.

4. Enter the name of the ESXi server you want to use as a source as well as valid credentials.

5. Select the virtual machine to convert. Make sure it has VMware tools installed. The VM can be either powered on or off.

6. Enter a workspace folder to store the converted disk.

7. Wait for the process to finish.

8. You will have the following screen:

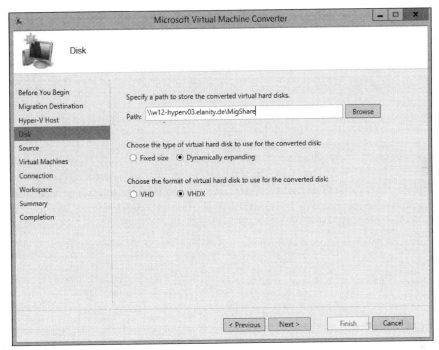

The Microsoft Virtual Machine Converter

There is some additional guidance available here: `http://bit.ly/1vBqjOU`.

This is a great and easy way to migrate a single virtual machine. Repeat the steps for every other virtual machine you have, or use some automation.

Microsoft Automation Toolkit

If you have a number of virtual machines to convert, the **Microsoft Automation Toolkit (MAT)** is a great choice. It adds a layer of automation above MVMC and can be downloaded from `http://bit.ly/XyLgeG`.

MAT is a collection of PowerShell scripts that automate conversions using the MVMC. It's backended by current versions of a SQL Server (SQL Express will work). You can use it to convert several machines at once, on a single server or across many servers at once. The automation options of MAT can be extended to a fully customized end-to-end solution. However, even in a fully automated environment, the conversion will take a lot of time. All virtual disks must be converted in a V2V conversion by all common tools. This takes time on a single virtual disk and a lot of time on multiple virtual disks. The time directly correlates to the size of the virtual disks as well.

Some additional guidance on MAT can be found here: `http://bit.ly/1B8tSf5`.

There is one solution available to speed up the conversion process, which we will discuss in the next section.

MAT powered by Project Shift

If you think of MAT as an add-on for MVMC, then MAT powered by Project Shift is another add-on on top of that. Project Shift enables hardware-accelerated conversions of virtual disks. It converts virtual disks located on a NetApp storage controller between formats at amazing speeds. It can convert between several formats but the most interesting is the VMDK to VHD conversion. For example, I was able to convert a 40 GB VMDK to a VHDX by using the PowerShell cmdlet:

```
ConvertTo-NaVhd
```

This conversion took about 6 seconds. As of today, this only works on NetApp storage controller because the NetApp controller simply repoints the data from the VMDK into a Hyper-V VHD, writing the appropriate metadata as it progresses. The resulting file is a VHD or VHDX file that takes up practically no extra space on disk and is finished in seconds. While NetApp Shift is available on a NetApp filer, it does not allow for whole VM conversions. This is why Microsoft combined it with MAT to build—again—an end-to-end conversion experience.

MAT powered by Project Shift scales extremely well and is the first choice of tool for a migration for hundreds of virtual machines. It is so successful that I have seen customers running other storage systems borrowing the NetApp filer to leverage these hardware-assisted conversions. A Mat-powered Project Shift conversion is shown in the following diagram:

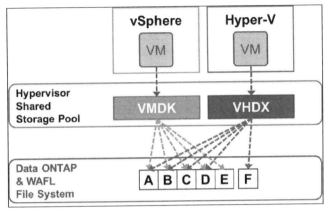

MAT powered by Project Shift

Some additional guidance can be found here: `http://bit.ly/1tRiMcc`.

Other V2V scenarios

There are a bunch of other tools available in the market for V2V conversions. The 5nine easy converter and the StarWind V2V converter offer a very similar experience to the MVMC + MAT solution accelerators, but can add particular value needed in advanced migration scenarios.

There is one tool in particular that can add real value to the shown conversion scenarios: the Double-take Move by Vision Solution offers a lot more out-of-the-box automation options, such as integration with System Center Orchestrator and Service Manager, and comes with superior capabilities, such as replicating running VMware VMs to Hyper-V. However, it comes with a price—literally. It is not free and requires a license per migrated virtual machine. Use Double-take Move if money is not your most valuable resource and you are looking for a fully automated conversion experience.

All mentioned tools are focused on moving from VMware to Hyper-V. What if you have virtual machines running on Citrix XenServer?

Citrix offers a free tool called XenConvert, which can be found at `http://bit.ly/WXrnhd`, and it allows for a conversion of XenServer VMs into the OVF format. The OVF format is just a container format hosting the XenServer VM configuration and its virtual hard drive in a VHD format. This conversion can be done with the following steps:

1. Create a new virtual machine in Hyper-V.
2. Attach the VHD file found in the OVF container.
3. Boot up the virtual machine.
4. Upgrade its integration services and you are done.

Some additional guidance can be found at `http://bit.ly/Y4c2Mn`.

If you have virtual machines running on any other Hypervisor than vSphere or Citrix, treat the VM the same way you would treat physical server systems.

Physical to Virtual conversions

While server virtualization is common in Enterprise data center, most of my customers are still running some physical server systems for legacy reasons. Those workloads can be transferred to virtual machines as well with **Physical to Virtual (P2V)** conversions.

Again, there are several tools available on the market to accomplish this task, including the new MVMC 3.0, SCVMM 2012 SP1 (the R2 Version dropped P2V support in favor of MVMC 3.0), and Disc2VHD. P2V conversions are very complex tasks offering a lot of complexity. To my personal surprise, the tool with the highest success rate of all P2V conversions done at Elanity Customers is not the most evolved tool—it's the simplest.

Disc2VHD is started on the physical system you want to convert. Stop all databases and services involved in your server workloads and let Disc2VHD do its work. It will create a VSS snapshot and create a VHDX file on a per block level from the physical disk and its partition. Just attach this create VHDX file, which is bootable, to a newly created Hyper-V VM. This is very simple but most efficient. This is shown in the following screenshot:

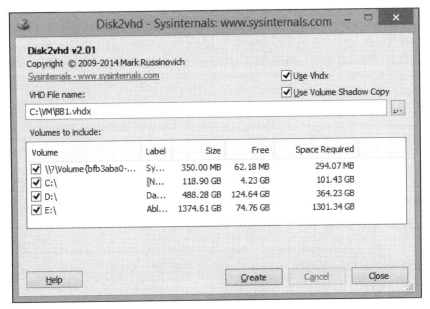

Disc2VHD

Like most P2V solutions, there is some cleaning to be done afterwards to remove old physical drivers from the system. While I highly recommend removing network and local printer drivers from the VM, I have not seen any harm done by another kind of driver.

To remove a driver from a device no longer connected to the system, a special view of **Device Manager** is necessary. Open a command prompt as administrator and run the following commands:

```
set DEVMGR_SHOW_NONPRESENT_DEVICES=1

devmgmt.msc
```

A **Device Manager** window opens, navigate to **View | Show hidden Devices | Network adapters** and right-click on any grayed-out items and select **Uninstall**. Repeat the same process for a local printer if installed and make sure to reboot the system afterwards. Your system is afterwards production-ready. Some additional guidance can be found at http://bit.ly/1mbMfKj.

Note that there are no experiences yet with MVMC 3.0, being just released around the same time as this book.

Virtualizing domain controllers

The last best practice I want to give you is about moving special workloads to Hyper-V. After having done many P2V migrations, there are only two workloads that deserve the attribute "special": a small business server and a domain controller. The first one is very simple—don't try to convert small business servers, they are outdated. Create a new virtual machine and rebuild the services offered by SBS with the current products. If you will get rid of the SBS server in the process, every IT person will love you.

The second one deserves a special consideration. Is it a good idea to virtualize domain controllers? Absolutely, they are built for it. Should you convert physical domain controllers? If you have to, you can do it. Often, it is faster to just deploy a new DC to the existing domain and remove the old one after that from the domain.

Should you virtualize all your domain controllers? Absolutely not. Domain controllers run great in virtual machines; however, due to problems related to time synchronization and a chicken/egg problem related to Hyper-V hosts hosting their own DCs, you should still place one physical domain controller per domain. While it is absolutely possible to overcome this limitation and virtualize the last domain controller too, it's often not worth the hassle and therefore not the best practice.

Additional information on this topic can be found at `http://bit.ly/1q06ygi`.

Summary

After finishing this book with this last chapter, you have read a lot about Hyper-V best practices. You have learned about faster Hyper-V deployment, High Availability options, and disaster recovery scenarios. You have seen the most relevant best practices around storage, network, and performance tuning. You have read overviews about central management with System Center for Hyper-V, and last but not least, you know how to move the existing services to Hyper-V. This all can only come to one conclusion: your Hyper-V skills are now ready for production!

Index

Thank you for buying
Hyper-V Best Practices

About Packt Publishing

Packt, pronounced 'packed', published its first book "*Mastering phpMyAdmin for Effective MySQL Management*" in April 2004 and subsequently continued to specialize in publishing highly focused books on specific technologies and solutions.

Our books and publications share the experiences of your fellow IT professionals in adapting and customizing today's systems, applications, and frameworks. Our solution based books give you the knowledge and power to customize the software and technologies you're using to get the job done. Packt books are more specific and less general than the IT books you have seen in the past. Our unique business model allows us to bring you more focused information, giving you more of what you need to know, and less of what you don't.

Packt is a modern, yet unique publishing company, which focuses on producing quality, cutting-edge books for communities of developers, administrators, and newbies alike. For more information, please visit our website: www.packtpub.com.

About Packt Enterprise

In 2010, Packt launched two new brands, Packt Enterprise and Packt Open Source, in order to continue its focus on specialization. This book is part of the Packt Enterprise brand, home to books published on enterprise software – software created by major vendors, including (but not limited to) IBM, Microsoft and Oracle, often for use in other corporations. Its titles will offer information relevant to a range of users of this software, including administrators, developers, architects, and end users.

Writing for Packt

We welcome all inquiries from people who are interested in authoring. Book proposals should be sent to author@packtpub.com. If your book idea is still at an early stage and you would like to discuss it first before writing a formal book proposal, contact us; one of our commissioning editors will get in touch with you.

We're not just looking for published authors; if you have strong technical skills but no writing experience, our experienced editors can help you develop a writing career, or simply get some additional reward for your expertise.

Hyper-V Replica Essentials

ISBN: 978-1-78217-188-1   Paperback: 96 pages

Ensure business continuity and improve your disaster recovery policy using Hyper-V Replica

1. A practical step-by-step guide that goes beyond theory and focuses on getting hands-on experience.

2. Ensure business continuity and faster disaster recovery.

3. Learn how to deploy a failover cluster and encrypt communication traffic.

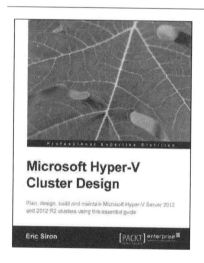

Microsoft Hyper-V Cluster Design

ISBN: 978-1-78217-768-5   Paperback: 462 pages

Plan, design, build and maintain Microsoft Hyper-V Server 2012 and 2012 R2 clusters using this essential guide

1. Successfully deploy a Microsoft Hyper-V Server clusteruse the right tools for building and maintaining a Hyper-V clusterMaster the intricacies of Hyper-V Server in a clustered environment.

Please check **www.PacktPub.com** for information on our titles

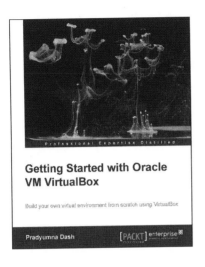

Getting Started with Oracle VM VirtualBox

ISBN: 978-1-78217-782-1   Paperback: 86 pages

Build your own virtual environment from scratch using VirtualBox

1. Learn how to install, configure, and manage VirtualBox.

2. A step-by-step guide which will teach you how to build your own virtual environment from scratch.

3. Discover advanced features of VirtualBox.

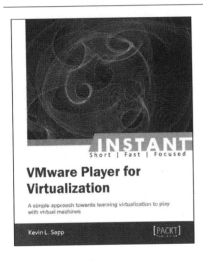

Instant VMware Player for Virtualization

ISBN: 978-1-84968-984-7   Paperback: 84 pages

A simple approach towards learning virtualization to play with virtual machines

1. Learn something new in an Instant! A short, fast, focused guide delivering immediate results.

2. Discover the latest features of VMware Player 5.0.

3. Evaluate new technology without paying for additional hardware costs.

4. Test your applications in an isolated environment.

Please check **www.PacktPub.com** for information on our titles

Made in the USA
San Bernardino, CA
11 May 2015